MOM'S LONG
GOODBYE

LINDA BRENDLE

MOM'S LONG GOODBYE by Linda Brendle

ANAIAH INSPIRATIONS
An imprint of ANAIAH PRESS, LLC.
7780 49th ST N. #129
Pinellas Park, FL 33781

First Anaiah Inspirations print edition March 2019

ISBN 978-1-947327-45-0

Anaiah
✝ Press
Books that Inspire

To David Pearson Brendle,
the amazing man
who spent the first twelve years of our marriage
walking this long and winding road with me

And to the One who brought us together

ACKNOWLEDGEMENTS

No book makes it to print without the help of friends, family, and various professionals who offer emotional, spiritual, moral, and technical support as well as creative space. Since Mom's Long Goodbye was written as the events happened, I owe my greatest thanks to those who helped me survive caring for Mom and Dad and saying goodbye to both of them.

There are too many to name, but here are a few:

My husband, David, who gave up so much during those years; my son, Christian, and daughter-in-law, Amy; my brother, Jim, and sister-in-law, Jo Lynn; my friend Mary; and my aunt, Fay, all of whom were only a phone call away when I needed them; and my friend Sue Brown, her husband, Willard, and the members of our caregiver support group. I am also grateful to the readers of A Long and Winding Road who wanted to know the rest of the story and to Eden Plantz, Kara Leigh Miller, Melinda Dozier, and the rest of the wonderful staff at Anaiah Press who gave me the opportunity to share that story and this one. It is my hope that Mom's story and mine will offer some relief, encouragement, and comfort to those whose story is not yet complete and those who are grieving.

2 Corinthians 1:3-5 (KJV)
3Blessed be God, even the Father of our Lord Jesus Christ, the Father of mercies, and the God of all comfort;
4Who comforteth us in all our tribulation, that we may be able to comfort them which are in any trouble, by the comfort wherewith we ourselves are comforted of God.
5For as the sufferings of Christ abound in us, so our consolation also aboundeth by Christ.

PROLOGUE
You Say Goodbye, but You Don't Go Away

Genesis 24:56 (KJV) *And he said unto them, Hinder me not, seeing the Lord hath prospered my way; send me away that I may go to my master.*

Some people have a hard time saying goodbye. There are the false-start types. When it's time to leave, they say, "I'd better get on home now." They stand in the doorway, keys in hand, and talk for another fifteen minutes. Sometimes, it takes them several more attempts before they actually make it out the door.

There are also the revolving-door types. They make it out the door quickly enough, but they pop back in several times to retrieve something they forgot or to tell you one more thing. I tend toward the second type, and I have a friend who finds it amusing. On my second or third round trip back, she smiles knowingly and says, "You say goodbye, but you don't go away."

There's another type of person who takes a long time to say goodbye. It's not a loveable personality trait that makes them linger in the doorway to tell you just one more thing or a quirky forgetfulness that makes it difficult to leave. Instead, it's tangled knots of nerves in their brain that become encrusted with plaque and steal them away from their loved ones a piece at a time. Mom was one of those people. She had Alzheimer's, and it took her fifteen years to say goodbye.

SECTION I
Grieving

CHAPTER 1
Fear and the Red Photo Album

2 Timothy 1:7 *For God hath not given us the spirit of fear; but of power, and of love, and of a sound mind.*

Mom was afraid for a long time. I found evidence of her fear in an old, red photo album, the kind with a thick cardboard cover bound with braided cord. It had a rose embossed on the front, and I sat on the floor, wondering what forgotten pictures were inside. Instead of pictures, there were articles. Page after page of neatly clipped and mounted stories about dementia and Alzheimer's. Stories of symptoms, stories of promising theories, stories with more questions than answers, stories of Mom's first steps into the darkness.

*****

Mom was always a fearful person, especially when she was alone. Dad worked nights several times during their seventy-year marriage. She sometimes told the story of being a young bride, left alone in an isolated country house while her groom worked at the ice house every night. One evening, she was awakened from a restless sleep by a terrible noise. She later described it as sounding like someone was trying to get into the house straight through the wall of her bedroom. She had no phone and no close neighbors, so she huddled in the center of the bed, trembling with fear and wondering how long she had left to live.

The noise continued for a while, but when the walls didn't splinter and the threat didn't seem to increase, she screwed up her courage and crept outside to investigate. She slipped down the front steps and peeked around the corner, and there, she saw it. An old milk cow was chewing on the grass that grew up beside the pier and beam foundation that supported the house. She laughed about it after the fact, but she and I had a replay of sorts years later when I was in my early teens.

We lived in the city by then, and Dad still worked nights, this time at the post office. My older brother, Jim, was away at college, so Mom and I were on our own. I was sound asleep when I was awakened by an urgent whisper.

"Linda! Come in here. Somebody's trying to get in the window."

I jumped up and ran into her room. She was sitting up in bed, her back pressed against the headboard with the covers drawn up to her chin.

"There," she said, pointing to the window beside her pillow. "Somebody was scratching on the screen."

I sat on the side of the bed for a minute, staring at the window. The closed window shade was backlit by a full moon and gave off an eerie glow. Suddenly, a shadow passed across the window, and I scooted under the covers and into Mom's arms. We sat that way for a few minutes, but when there was no further movement or sound, curiosity overcame fear, and I slid out of bed and tiptoed to the window. I pulled the shade away just far enough to peek out.

"I don't see anything. I'm going to call Dad."

Without turning on a light, I went to the phone that sat in its recessed nook in the hallway wall. All the modern houses had them. Like a blind person reading Braille, I slid my fingers over the dial, counted the holes, and dialed the number.

"Dad, I think somebody's trying to get in. Something was scratching on the screen in your bedroom, and I saw a shadow on the shade."

"Did you look out?"

"Yes, I peeped out and couldn't see anyone."

"Okay. Stay away from the window. I'm going to call the police."

"Okay."

Within minutes, we heard a car pull up in front of the house and saw the beams of flashlights as Mesquite's finest investigated. Then, we heard a knock on the door.

"We didn't find anything, Ma'am, but we'll have a patrol car drive by here frequently for the rest of the night."

When Dad got home the next morning, he found us still huddled together under the covers. He immediately went out to investigate; he was laughing when he came back inside.

"I didn't find any footprints or anything, but I did find some evidence. There were rat droppings on the window sill."

We took a bit of kidding about being afraid of the dark, but Mom wasn't just afraid of things that go bump in the night. She was afraid in the daylight, too. She was afraid of making a mistake, afraid of looking foolish in front of others, of being embarrassed, of being looked down on.

She had a beautiful voice and helped lead the singing in her tiny, country church when she was a teenager. That was before air conditioning, when church windows actually opened and congregations cooled themselves with cardboard fans provided by the local funeral home. One Sunday morning, a fly flew in an open window and straight into Mom's mouth as she sang. She was so embarrassed she became reluctant to lead the singing. Not long after that, she learned that the former song leader had been diagnosed with throat cancer. Fearful that his singing might have contributed to his illness, she retired from her leadership position and rejoined the congregation.

She had other musical talents, too. She learned to play the guitar by watching her uncles when the kinfolks gathered for a songfest, and she also played the piano by ear. We had an old player piano we inherited from one relative or another. The player mechanics had been removed, Dad had refinished it, and Mom spent many happy hours playing honky-tonk tunes and old gospel favorites. When we

3

moved from a small West Texas town into the suburbs of Dallas, though, she feared that city folks would look down on her country origins, so she did her best to cover them up. Her guitar was relegated to the back of her closet, and the piano was made available for me to practice the Old Masters favored by my piano teacher.

Mom also feared illness and physical infirmities of all kinds. She was born with yellow jaundice, as it was known in the country, and she was sickly as a child. As an adult, she endured a tonsillectomy, an appendectomy, a hysterectomy, three spinal fusions, and the removal of a deformed kidney, so she saved her best nightgowns for her next trip to the hospital. She feared falling victim to any epidemic or new disease that made the rounds of the morning talk shows. In spite of her fear, or maybe because of it, she often developed the symptoms of those diseases. What she feared most, though, was Alzheimer's. I didn't realize how much until I found that old photo album.

Mom and Dad lived with us for six years before they went into assisted living. By that time, neither of them was capable of making the decisions necessary in downsizing. I went through their personal belongings and made piles: things to pack, things to store, things to donate, things to throw away. I found trash, and I found treasures— and I found the photo album in the bottom of one of Mom's dresser drawers. I wonder how long she lived alone with her fear before the rest of us suspected.

CHAPTER 2
Denial, Anger, and Conversational Loops

Proverbs 12:18 *There is that speaketh like the piercings of a sword: but the tongue of the wise is health.*

There is no way to measure all the pain of Alzheimer's or to say what aspect of the disease is the hardest to face, but one of the more difficult is the grieving of a loss that hasn't ended. As a caregiver, I went through denial, anger, bargaining, depression, acceptance: all the classic stages of grief. The first stages were by far the ugliest.

Mom's memory started to fail fifteen years before she died. My role as her caregiver began with an occasional offer of assistance—*Here, Mom, let me help you with that*—and progressed to holding her hand and searching for any sign of response in her eyes. My reactions to her first symptoms weren't nearly as gentle and understanding as my last ones were. Denial takes many forms, and sometimes, those forms are not very pretty.

Her first obvious symptom was what I call conversational loops, telling the same story or asking the same questions three or four times in fifteen minutes. Since she had a penchant for contracting every disease she read about in the newspaper or saw on TV, she came down with whatever flu was making the rounds each year. When she was bitten by a tick at a family reunion, she was not diagnosed with Lyme disease, but she developed all the symptoms. She was even convinced that she had AIDS since she had received blood transfusions in the past, but when her doctor told her one of the first symptoms was a drastic weight loss, she decided she didn't have it after all. As a result of her history, and because I didn't want to believe it, I told myself that her memory issues were another expression of her fear. I told myself she was acting forgetful because that's the way she thought a person of her age should act.

I wasn't the only one who was stuck in denial; Dad didn't want to believe it either. It was rare that I was alone with him. Mom's possessiveness of her faithful husband extended to everyone, even me, and she also wanted to be sure she didn't miss anything. However, one day when I dropped by for a lunch-time visit, she was still fixing her hair, so I had a few minutes to talk with him.

"Dad, does Mom talk in loops when it's just the two of you?"

"What do you mean?"

I explained what I meant, and he said, "Oh, that. Yeah, she does it sometimes."

"Do you think she's just not paying attention, or is it something more serious?"

"I think she's just not paying attention."

Even Mom's primary care doctor seemed to be in denial about the possibility of major memory problems. He was my doctor, too, so I felt comfortable enough with him to make an appointment to sit down and talk about what was going on.

"So, what do you think?" I asked. "Do you think the loops and other lapses are the beginning of something bigger, and if so, what can we do?"

"I think there may be a little something going on," he said. "But I don't think we're looking at Alzheimer's or anything like that. Even if we were, there's not much that can be done. There are a couple of medications available, but they don't cure it. They only slow down the symptoms temporarily. There are significant side effects, and after a few months, you're right back where you started."

What he didn't share with me, probably because of patient confidentiality, and what Mom and Dad didn't tell me, probably because my family has never been big on discussing uncomfortable issues, was that she had already tried and rejected those medications and their side effects. The subject of her failing memory wasn't discussed openly for a while after that, and I continued to deny and stew in silence—and sometimes, my worry bubbled out in some very unattractive ways.

Around the time Mom's symptoms became noticeable, I met Mary. We both sang alto in the church choir, and that was only one of many things we had in common. We were both single again, we each had one child who was having some coming-of-age difficulties, we laughed and cried at the same TV shows, and we became soul sisters. Mom and Dad loved her, too, and they called her their second daughter. Mary has the gift of mercy, and she was more patient than I was. When Mom started her looping conversations, Mary made a game of it.

"I see how many different ways I can answer the same question truthfully," she said.

I wasn't nearly as compassionate; I was angry. Denial and anger do not make a pretty pair. As a classic, textbook codependent, I needed control of my life in order to feel safe, and what I saw in Mom was beyond my control. Even though I had been through lots of counseling and was learning to set boundaries and live my own life, seeing Mom begin to slip away rocked my world, and I didn't like it. I was frustrated and scared, and since I couldn't get at the disease, I vented at Mom.

"I just told you that two minutes ago, Mom," or "You've told me that three times in the last ten minutes."

Not my proudest moments. One afternoon, when Dad was in the hospital and I was helping her get ready to go see him, I snapped at her about some trivial irritant. She was still aware enough at that point to understand some of what was happening, even though she was powerless to control it. She looked at me with hurt in her eyes.

"You don't have to make me feel bad about it."

I don't have to tell you how small I felt and how much I wish I could take back all the harsh things I said to her during those months.

CHAPTER 3
Bargaining and the "A" Word

Joshua 2:12–13 *12Now therefore, I pray you, swear unto me by the Lord, since I have shewed you kindness, that ye will also shew kindness unto my father's house, and give me a true token: 13And that ye will save alive my father, and my mother, and my brethren, and my sisters, and all that they have, and deliver our lives from death.*

There comes a point when even an ostrich has to pull her head out of the sand and look at the world around her. When I could no longer deny what was happening, I began to bargain. I didn't do the "God, if You'll heal her, I'll do XYZ" kind of bargaining—I tried to fix it. If I could just find the right doctor, the right medicine, the right kind of assistance. Unfortunately, as all Alzheimer's caregivers know, no matter how good a job you do, your loved one won't get better. This insidious disease will wrap their minds in plaque-covered nerve tangles until they forget what you told them, they forget who you are, they forget how to care for themselves, and eventually, they forget how to breathe.

After my unproductive visit with Mom's primary care doctor, I began to look for other options. I did some internet research, but the facts were too harsh, and I was still too deep in my denial to accept much of it. Talking with friends who also had aging parents was a gentler option, so I talked, and I listened. One of my friends was caring for her husband who had a mysterious kind of aphasia and was losing his ability to communicate. I pumped her for information about his symptoms, his treatment, and his doctors. She was taking him to a treatment facility with an impressive-sounding name and a doctor with equally impressive credentials. Surely, I'd find help there.

I broke the family code of silence and called my brother in Arkansas to discuss the situation. Since he was not around Mom as much as I was, he was still in the denial stage, but after hearing more details about what was going on, he agreed that the situation needed some attention. I set up an appointment, Jim made arrangements to come to Texas, and we arrived at the doctor's office en masse.

The doctor was very understanding. He allowed all of us—Dad, Jim, and me—to accompany Mom into the examining room. He checked the blood flow in her arteries, he checked reflexes, and he asked questions. It was the first time I'd heard a doctor ask a patient to spell "world" backward, but it wasn't the last. Mom seemed totally at ease, basking in the attention of the doctor—she'd always had a thing for men in white lab coats. Then, the tests were over, and it was time for him to give us his opinion. He used the "A" word.

"I want to set up an MRI so I can get a look at her brain, but I'm pretty sure we're dealing with Alzheimer's."

He went on for a bit about stages and treatments and what to expect, but I didn't hear much of it. That word echoed in my head and drowned out everything else. We left with prescriptions and appointments and the beginning of the depression that sets in when you can no longer deny the truth.

My caregiving duties, which up to that point had consisted of occasional social and check-in visits, began to increase. I began to visit Mom and Dad daily, and my gentle reminders to carry out simple personal and housekeeping tasks evolved into hands-on intervention.

I continued to watch Mom slide down the slippery slope into forgetfulness, and there wasn't a thing I could do about it. I could no longer deny what was happening. I was still angry, and bargaining didn't work—and then our lives turned upside-down.

CHAPTER 4
Plans, Change, and Anxiety

Proverbs 16:9 *A man's heart deviseth his way: but the LORD directeth his steps.*

We didn't plan to move to Florida, but apparently, the Lord had other plans. On a beautiful September day in 2004, I wrecked my motorcycle, David heard the news that his job in Dallas was coming to an end, and Dad took a fall that confirmed my growing feeling that I needed to be even more involved in his and Mom's lives. Sometimes, change comes suddenly.

David had been working as a scheduler in the Delta Airlines maintenance hangar at the Dallas-Fort Worth Airport. The news was the DFW hangar was closing, and if he wanted to keep his job, we would need to relocate. After much prayer and research, we made the difficult decision to move to the Tampa Bay area and to take Mom and Dad with us. Convincing them to come along was even more difficult.

Initially, they refused to even consider the possibility, but after some tough love persuasion from me, they finally agreed to pull up their lifelong Texas roots. Once the decision was made, Dad covered any feelings he had with his typical stoicism. Mom was a little more volatile. Sometimes, she was excited about a new home and someone to take over the cooking duties which had become too much for her. At other times, she was terrified that we were taking her to Florida to put her in a nursing home.

The transition went smoothly, considering the circumstances, and Mom put on a happy face, seeming to enjoy our new home and living circumstances. However, there was trouble below the surface.

Occasionally, when she thought I was out of earshot, she would whisper to Dad in conspiratorial tones. Soon afterward, he would march into the kitchen or wherever I happened to be and announce that they were packing up their car and heading back to Texas. Having been through the Terrible Twos with my son, though, I was familiar with the tactic of distraction.

"Is that right?" I would respond calmly. "Why don't you wait until tomorrow morning so you can get an early start. It's a really long trip."

"Okay," he would say, and he'd go back to their TV room to relate the news to Mom, assuming he remembered it that long.

By the time I had dinner on the table, she would be back in good spirits or would have found something else to worry about. One of her other fears was that Dad was cheating on her. She imagined that he was getting phone calls from girls he knew in high school, and if he was not where she could see him, she sometimes thought he was on a hot date. Fortunately, the doctors in Florida are familiar with the infirmities of old age, and her new neurologist knew just what to prescribe to eliminate the delusions and lessen the anxiety. Unfortunately, with my new role as a full-time caregiver, along with my ringside seat to the ravages of Alzheimer's and dementia, I was raising a whole new crop of anxieties of my own.

CHAPTER 5
Another Kind of Fear—Spelling 'World' Backward

John 9:2–3 *²And his disciples asked him, saying, Master, who did sin, this man, or his parents, that he was born blind? ³Jesus answered, Neither hath this man sinned, nor his parents: but that the works of God should be made manifest in him.*

My husband, David, worries about his failing memory. I think it's simply one of the typical signs of aging exhibited by those of us in the Baby Boomer generation. Still, when he struggles to remember an elusive name or movie title, he worries that it might be something more serious.

"Linda, I can't remember anything anymore. My memory is getting terrible."

"Can you spell 'world' backward?"

The first time I responded that way, he looked at me like I was a few sandwiches shy of a picnic, but after more than a decade together, he was accustomed to my little tangents.

"D-L-R-O-W. Right?"

"Right. You're okay."

Of course, the memory tests the neurologist gave Mom included much more than that one question. If I recall, it went something like this.

"Mrs. Robinson, do you know what day of the week it is?"

"Tuesday?" It wasn't.

"Do you know what month it is?"

"September?" That was wrong, too, but her birthday is in September, and it's her favorite month.

"What season is it?"

"Spring?" I guess that's another favorite.

"I'm going to name three objects, and I want you to remember them. I'll ask you to tell me what they are a little later. Ready? A ball, a flag, and a tree. Got that?"

Probably not.

"What city are we in? County? State?"

Planet?

"I want you start with 100 and count backward by 7."

You're kidding, right?

After a few more unanswerable questions, he went back to the three objects and got the expected response.

"What three objects?"

Then came the big finale, "Can you spell 'world' backward?"

Of course not.

Excited as she was by all the attention, Mom usually missed the moments when the doctor used the dreaded "A" word, that strange word that strikes fear into the hearts of the bravest of us. For a while, we were careful not to use the word in front of her. If she heard it and realized it was being applied to her, she went into hysterics, sobbing out her greatest fears.

"I don't want to end up like Mama. I'd rather die than live like that."

Over the next several years, I listened to various doctors administer the same tests, or slight variations thereof. Mom's answers deteriorated to the point where she no longer even tried to answer, often turning to me, asking me to answer the questions for her. During her last few appointments, the doctor greeted Mom and asked how she was feeling. Then, he turned to me to find out how she was really doing.

One of the few good things about her downward slide was that, the further down she went, the less terror the "A" word held for her. I can't say the same for myself.

Mom's mother died of Alzheimer's, and two of her sisters suffered from it. As if that weren't enough, Dad had vascular dementia. It seems like the deck is stacked against me. I've done a little research on the disease, but not too much. I know that progress is being made, but right now, there's no cure and no treatments that are really very effective. It's kind of like how sausage is made—you don't really want to know the details. Still, I know that keeping your body healthy and your mind active are important, so I do that—and so far, I can still spell 'world' backward.

SECTION II
Initial Changes

CHAPTER 6
What Is That Smell

Ezekiel 36:25 *Then will I sprinkle clean water upon you, and ye shall be clean.*

After the visit with the neurologist, it became more difficult to deny the increasing changes in Mom's habits and behaviors, especially considering the results of some of those changes. The hardest result to deny was the smell.

When he was seven years old, my grandson, Mattias, asked his dad a question: *Dad, how come, when people get older, they smell a little bit worse?* That's a question that came up a lot in the caregiver support group at our church. As group facilitator, I tried to find answers and even resorted to the internet. The consensus on several websites was that there isn't an overall reason for that "old" smell, like an aging cellular structure or elderly pheromones. Some articles attributed the smell to oral medications or topical ointments, but most agreed that the biggest culprit is poor hygiene, both personal and household.

I learned more than I wanted to know about those poor hygiene practices and the reasons behind them during the six years Mom and Dad lived with us. When we moved to Florida, we chose a house with a split plan so each couple could have their private space. Mom and Dad's "apartment," as she liked to call it, consisted of a sitting area, two bedrooms, and two bathrooms. At first, I stayed out of their area except for occasional visits. I told myself it was out of respect for their privacy, but there was some avoidance involved, too. Most of our together time was at meals and in the den after dinner when we all watched TV. I left the housekeeping of their apartment to them, telling myself that they needed the feeling of independence that came with the responsibility. However, after a few months, unpleasant odors began to creep out their door and permeate the rest of the house. I encouraged them to bathe and clean their rooms more often, but I met the kind of resistance you get from a rebellious teenager. I was frustrated at what seemed like a lazy, stubborn refusal to improve the situation.

Then, in 2007, we took our infamous RV trip. Spending seven weeks in extremely close proximity opened my eyes to some of the reasons behind their refusal. First of all, their memories were much worse than I realized, and they didn't remember that it had been several days since they bathed or changed their bed or cleaned their toilet. In addition, as people age, they become much less sensitive to the world around them. One of the first senses to go is often the sense of smell. To put it simply, Mom and Dad were not aware they smelled bad.

There was also an element of fear in their reluctance. Dad was very unsteady on his feet, so stepping in and out of a bathtub was a daunting task. The small shower in the RV with its built-in seat and handheld sprayer seemed to work pretty well, so when we returned home, I changed his bath venue to our bathroom with its walk-in shower. He was, if not enthusiastic, at least more compliant. That worked for a while, but one day, he fell in the shower, and we had to go back to his bathroom. We installed a handheld sprayer, a bath seat, a nonslip mat, and two grab bars. Before every bath, I instructed him on safe entrance into and exit from the tub and prayed until he appeared a while later, clean and safe. He sometimes skipped the shampoo, but I took into consideration that his arthritic shoulder probably made washing his hair painful, and I didn't make an issue of it.

Mom seemed afraid of bath time because of the vulnerability she felt being naked and alone. During our trip, I became aware that she was also confused about turning the water on and off and controlling the temperature. I began staying in the bathroom with her to offer encouragement and support, and she did much better. She continued to do well in our shower when we got home, but although she never fell, she got almost as unsteady on her feet as Dad. When their bathroom got its safety makeover, I moved her back there. The process had become so confusing for her, that I bathed her. I usually ended up with water all over the floor and myself and, more often than not, an aching back. It was hard for me emotionally as well as physically, but Mom enjoyed the attention, and I enjoyed the result, so I kept at it.

Toward the end of our RV trek, we visited my brother for a few days and left Mom and Dad with him while we drove the rest of the way home by ourselves. It gave Jim some quality time with his parents, and it gave David and me some quality time with each other. When we got home, I took the opportunity to do some deep cleaning on Mom and Dad's side of the house. It was an "aha" moment. The bed hadn't been changed for way too long, partly because of lack of awareness of the need, but also because weak and painful backs made the process difficult. Following the odor trails, I found dirty clothes in the closets, both in piles on the floor and on hangers. I found more dirty clothes in drawers. The only way to separate the clean clothes from the dirty was the unpleasant sniff test, so I washed everything!

After the trip, I tried to be a little more understanding and a little less irritable. Like a mother training her young children, I became very involved in the hygiene routines. I laid out clean clothes, I put toothpaste on the toothbrushes, I supervised regular bath days and bath routines, I included Mom and Dad's side of the house in my cleaning routines, and I regularly searched for dirty clothes. The results were good and bad. The house and its residents smelled much better, but the added work pushed me more quickly toward caregiver burnout.

CHAPTER 7
Wardrobe Malfunctions

1 Timothy 2:9 *In like manner also, that women adorn themselves in modest apparel, with shamefacedness and sobriety.*

Another change Mom went through was in her ability to dress herself. During Super Bowl XXXVIII in 2004, Janet Jackson had a wardrobe malfunction that made headlines for weeks, but when it came to wardrobe malfunctions, Janet Jackson didn't hold a candle to my mother. Janet had a single incident, but Mom had them on a regular basis.

Mom and Dad slept late, sometimes very late. The doctor said that, as long as it didn't interfere with their sleeping at night, to let them sleep. Still, like a worried mother, I occasionally put my ear to their door as I passed by. Every so often, when it was nearing lunch time and their breakfast was still on the table, I took more aggressive action. One morning, awake noises and voices began around noon, but when they still hadn't emerged by 12:30, I tapped gently on their door.

"Knock, knock," I said.

"Come on in," Dad said.

"Do you need help getting dressed?" I said.

One look answered my question. Mom was sitting on the edge of the bed dressed in panties, socks, tennis shoes, and a white mock turtle neck topped with a blue cable knit sweater. The white sweater was on backward with the zipper gaping open, and Dad was helping her add a third layer, a pink pullover. A pink long-sleeved T-shirt lay in reserve on the bed beside her.

"Mom, you've already got on two sweaters. Do you really need a third one?"

She looked down at the pink sweater in confusion.

"I don't know," she said.

"It seems like a little bit too much. Don't you agree, Dad?"

Dad looked at Mom in surprise as if he hadn't noticed the extra sweaters.

"I guess so. I hadn't thought about it."

"Why did you need so many?" I said as I helped her pull the pink sweater off.

Usually, asking why was futile, but sometimes, I was lucky and gained some useable information.

"They didn't cover…," she said, looking distressed and patting her bare legs.

"No, they don't cover your legs. You need to get some pants."

"That's what she was looking for," Dad said.

"My fault," I said, pulling pink sweat pants out of the closet. "I didn't lay out pants last night. Take your shoes off, and we'll fix it."

She slipped out of her shoes, which were on the wrong feet, and I noticed that her feet looked unusually fat. I knelt for a sock inspection and started peeling off layers. If you're a caregiver and you come up short a sock or two on laundry day, you might check your loved one's feet. Mom's record was four on one foot, but that day, there were only three on the right foot and two on the left. With the proper ratio of socks to feet restored, we were ready for the sweat pants, which she slipped on without incident.

"Now let's get those sweaters off," I said. The second layer went better with the pants than the first layer, and the normal undergarment had been omitted altogether, so we started from scratch. I peeled off both layers and grabbed a clean bra out of her drawer.

"I'm cold," Mom said.

"I know. I'll hurry." I held the bra for her, and she slipped her arms into the straps. I leaned around and fastened the hooks behind her. Under normal circumstances, whatever normal was, she pulled

21

the band of the bra down into place while I fastened it. That day she missed that step. The band rode up at armpit level and the cups were empty of their intended contents.

"Mom, I think you forgot to do your job," I said. She looked down and giggled, and we went through the procedure again, this time with more success.

After that, we got the white sweater on and zipped up the back and the shoes on the correct feet. By 1:00 pm, she was eating breakfast and I was proceeding with my day. I often became irritated or frustrated at having to stop what I was doing to help her dress or undress, but I knew there would come a day when that job would be over, and I would miss her terribly. I was right.

CHAPTER 8
Wal-Mart Antics

Proverbs 31:14 *She is like the merchants' ships; she bringeth her food from afar.*

Before Alzheimer's, Mom loved to shop. She and I used to haunt the mall on Saturday afternoon after completing our morning cleaning chores and before buying the groceries for the coming week. Our routine was temporarily interrupted when I got married, moved to the other side of Dallas, and took a full-time job. However, after a few years, I quit work to start a family, and we developed a new shopping routine. Wednesday was double-coupon day at the grocery store, so she picked me up early, and we made a day of it. We'd hit the mall, do lunch, and buy groceries in time for her to get home before rush-hour traffic clogged the highway.

I went back to work when my son, Christian, was four years old, so she had to make her Wednesday shopping excursions without me. After Dad retired, they wanted to be closer to us, so they moved to our side of town. She had adjusted her shopping routine over the years, but she still went out on Wednesdays. She left Dad at home, working in the yard or piddling in the garage, while she made the rounds of the discount stores in the small town where we lived. They were on a fixed income, so she didn't have a lot of money, but she hoarded her weekly allowance and watched the bargain racks for those just-gotta-have items. The one thing that didn't change, though, was the last stop of the day—the grocery store.

Alzheimer's changed all this. I was aware that her shopping trips were getting shorter, more often than not omitting the discount stores and going straight to the grocery store. Then, Dad started doing the shopping, and Mom didn't like it. She complained about him not wanting her to have any fun, not buying the right things, and generally being a mean old man. At the same time, she recounted stories of not being able to find the things she was looking for, of getting lost in the maze of the familiar aisles, of becoming overwhelmed with the process and walking out of the store, leaving her full cart behind.

By the time she and Dad moved in with us, our days of spending an afternoon at the mall were a distant memory, or more accurately, a lost memory. She still liked the idea of shopping, and she always wanted to go with me, but she didn't usually enjoy the reality of our trips to Wal-Mart.

I first became a big fan of Wal-Mart when we bought our motor home, and I was even more enthusiastic after I became a caregiver. We never overnighted on one of their parking lots like many RVers do, but we lunched there quite often. Wal-Mart parking lots are generally easy in and easy out, even for a forty-foot vehicle towing a car, so if we were close to one around noon, we pulled in. After we ate, one or the other of us invariably suggested that we run inside to pick up this or that. If we couldn't find it there, we probably didn't need it anyway.

After Mom and Dad came to live with us, it became the shopping place of choice because of the convenience. With The Kids in tow, one stop was usually all I could manage, and once again, if I couldn't find it at Wally World, I didn't need it. One side benefit I didn't consider at the time was the anecdotes the visits would provide.

Our first Christmas together, I asked Mom and Dad if they wanted to do their own Christmas shopping or if they wanted me to do it. After some discussion, they came to a decision.

"We want you to buy for Jim, Jo Lynn, and David, but we'll shop for you."

"That works for me."

"Okay, but you'll need to give us a list. We don't know what you want."

On the appointed day, I made sure they had the short list of simple suggestions I had written, and we set out. We arrived at the store where I got them a basket and pointed them in the right direction.

"I have some shopping of my own to do. When you get finished, wait for me on that bench by the front door. Do you need anything else?"

"No, we're fine."

Taking them at their word, I set out with my own list. Less than fifteen minutes later, I glanced toward the front door and saw The Kids sitting on the bench looking a little lost.

"Hi, are you okay?"

"Yeah, we're just tired."

"Did you finish your shopping?"

"No, we can't find the list. Can you buy something for us?"

That was the first but not the last time I bought my own Christmas present.

The longer they lived with me, the less excited they were about trips to Wal-Mart. The conversation when we pulled into the parking lot often went like this:

"Are you going to be very long?"

"No, I just have to pick up a few things."

"Then we'll just wait in the car."

The first time or two this happened, I left the keys in the car in case they wanted to roll the windows up or down or listen to the radio. One afternoon, I finished my shopping and was surprised that they were sitting by the door.

"Hi, did you think of something you needed to buy?"

"No, we got hot."

Once they were on their feet and headed toward the car, I envisioned the windows down and the doors open. Fortunately, the windows were up and the doors were locked. Unfortunately, the keys were still inside. After that, I made sure I had a spare key in my purse.

After a year or two in Florida, a Super Wal-Mart opened in town. It ultimately became part of Mom and Dad's exercise program. We'd pull into the parking lot, and the familiar conversation would begin.

"We'll just wait in the car if you're not going to be long."

"I need you to come in with me. I need to take your blood pressure. Dr. Stephans wants me to take it at least once a week."

They were pretty obedient when doctor's orders were concerned. It wasn't a long way from the handicapped parking to the front door, but the pharmacy, with its blood pressure machine, was in the middle of the store, so it was a pretty good hike. If I had a short list, they waited in the pharmacy until I finished, but if I had a longer list, I took them to the Subway in the front of the store. I bought them each a cookie and a cup of coffee, and they watched people until I was ready to go. The cookie may not have been what the doctor ordered, but at least they had to walk to get it.

After Mom and Dad moved into assisted living, David and I moved to the country where the nearest Wal-Mart was twenty miles away. At first, I insisted on going into town once a week, but as I became more familiar with the local stores and better at long-range planning, two or three weeks sometimes elapsed between trips. I still like the one-stop convenience, but the trips are not nearly as interesting without Mom and Dad.

CHAPTER 9
Peeing in a Bottle

Proverbs 17:28 *Even a fool, when he holdeth his peace, is counted wise: and he that shutteth his lips is esteemed a man of understanding.*

The reason Mom always picked me up for our Wednesday shopping trips was that I didn't have a car of my own until I became pregnant. It was actually toward the end of the pregnancy when I bought my VW Bug.

When we first began to talk about starting a family, I had concerns. I had been taking birth control pills for several years, and I had heard conflicting information about how that might affect me, so I decided to consult my OB/GYN. He was very nonchalant, almost as if he dealt with the subject every day.

"Just finish the cycle of pills you're on, and get pregnant. As long as you're feeling okay, come see me after you've missed your second period."

Have I mentioned I'm not good at waiting? When I wasn't pregnant the first month, I cried. The next month, when my friendly visitor didn't show up, I was ecstatic. I intended to wait until I was sure before telling anybody, but that's a secret that's hard to keep. As the time drew near to visit the doctor, I couldn't contain myself.

"Mom and Dad," I said one night after dinner at their house. "I have a surprise. I think I'm pregnant!"

The reaction was explosive: tears, smiles, hugs, kisses. They already had two grandsons whom they adored, but they lived in Oklahoma. This one was going to be close enough for them to get their hands on frequently. The look in their eyes told me that I wouldn't have to worry about babysitters, but Mom didn't want to wait until the baby arrived to become involved.

"Do you want me to take you to your doctor's appointment," she said.

"That would be great," I said. My husband was a salesman, and if he wasn't working, he wasn't earning. He was old-fashioned enough he didn't feel a need to be involved in the gestation process until the doctor came into the waiting room and announced whether it was a boy or a girl, so he didn't feel as if his place was being usurped.

I made my appointment on Wednesday so we could combine the doctor's visit with our lunch and shopping routine. When the big day came, Mom picked me up, sporting a smile almost too wide for her face. We chattered all the way to the doctor's office about maternity clothes, cribs, diapers, and other baby stuff. We sat nervously in the reception area, waiting for my name to be called, looking at the happy faces of the other women in the room, most with swollen bellies. When it was finally my turn, Mom stayed in the reception room. It must have seemed like an eternity to her, wondering what was going on.

When I came out some time later, I was beaming, flushed with the words *You're going to have a baby.* I was also a little overwhelmed with information, instructions, and expectations. I floated through the reception room, following the nurse's instructions to go to the front desk to make my next appointment. The receptionist suggested a date and time, I agreed, and she handed me a reminder card along with a small, clear, widemouthed bottle.

I've often said that, while I'm highly intelligent, I'm not always very smart. I am, however, smart enough to be aware of my deficiencies and to follow the advice given in Proverbs about keeping your mouth shut.

I had no idea what the bottle was for, so I kept quiet about it— but moms know. Mine looked at me with the smile that hadn't left her face all morning and with amused understanding in her eyes.

"You don't know what that's for, do you?" she said.

"No," I said. I looked away and felt the heat rising in my face.

"It's for a urine specimen," she said. "They'll want one every time you come in."

"Oh. I thought it was so I could carry my vitamins with me in my purse or something."

We shared a good mother/daughter laugh, and she patted my arm.

"That's okay," she said. "The first time I went to the doctor when I was pregnant with Jim, they told me to bring a urine specimen. They didn't give me a bottle or tell me how much they needed."

"So, how much did you take them?"

"All of it. I think I filled up a fruit jar."

We shared a lot of moments over the next few months and years. We even shared some more "bottle" moments at the doctor's office as she got older. One particular incident stands out. After the nurse drew blood, she asked for a urine sample. By that time, Mom was beyond understanding the finer points of securing a clean specimen, so I went into the restroom with her. Nothing happened. She tried but couldn't produce even a trickle, so we retired to the waiting room, and I began to try and tempt her with cool water in little cone-shaped cups.

"No, thanks. I'm not thirsty."

"I know, but you have to give them a urine sample before we can go eat breakfast. You're hungry, aren't you?"

She was always hungry, so she drank several cups of water.

"Do you think can tinkle now?"

"No, I don't need to go."

"Well, let's give it a try anyway."

I won't describe the details of what followed, except to say that holding a specimen cup for someone else is not something a person would normally do for a casual friend—and that we were ultimately successful. Sharing such an intimate experience could have been awkward and embarrassing, but if there's anything good about

Alzheimer's, it's that the normal inhibitions are gone, and things that at one time would have been humiliating, are now funny. Throughout my caregiving experience, God continually taught me there's nothing awkward or embarrassing about helping one of the least of these.

CHAPTER 10
Remembering

1 Corinthians 11:24 *And when he had given thanks, he brake it, and said, Take, eat: this is my body, which is broken for you: this do in remembrance of me.*

Communion, or the Lord's Supper as we call it in Texas, is a beautiful service observed in remembrance of Jesus' sacrifice for us, but remembering was not something Mom did very well. As her Alzheimer's advanced into the late stages, Communion became very confusing to her.

She grew up in the Baptist church where Communion was generally served once a quarter and on special occasions. The elements were passed by the deacons, and the congregation prayerfully held them until, following prayer and a word of meditation, everyone ate or drank communally.

My brother and my daughter-in-law are both ministers of the Christian Church (Disciples of Christ) where Communion is a part of every service, and the elements are taken individually. Mom spent several weeks a year with my brother, and she visited Christian and Amy when we did, which was as often as possible. The frequency of her DOC Communion experience, plus a defective memory and poor impulse control, made the Baptist method difficult for her. One Sunday morning when we had Communion in our home church, I tried to instruct her ahead of time.

"Mom, when they pass the bread, just take it and hold it," I whispered as the deacons started to make their way down the aisles.

"What?" she asked in a rather loud voice.

I repeated my instructions a little louder.

"Just take the bread and hold it," she repeated to Dad, loud enough for several rows around us to hear.

A minute later, when the plate was passed down our row, she took a bit of the cracker and promptly put it in her mouth.

When she noticed that everyone else was holding theirs, she announced, "I ate mine too soon."

"It's okay," I reassured her as I broke mine and gave her part of it.

The whole process was repeated when the juice was passed, but it's really hard to pour from one of those tiny cups to another without making a mess.

Considering my previous lack of success, the next time we had Communion, I opted to skip the instructions and just let her observe the sacrament in her own way, hoping it would lead to less confusion and a more worshipful experience for all concerned. As the deacons began their work and the harp played softly in the background, I bowed my head and remembered. I remembered Jesus and His love, and I also remembered previous Communion experiences.

Shortly before our wedding, my first husband announced he didn't feel he could attend the Baptist church. I felt that as long as we found a Christ-centered church where we could worship together, the name on the door wasn't important. We found a lovely Episcopal church close to our new home and went through confirmation classes. We finished the classes, and the Sunday came for our first Communion. I approached the altar and knelt at the rail, trying hard to focus on the meaning of what I was about to do but more than a little intimidated by the unfamiliar ritual. The priest placed the wafer in my waiting hands, blessing it with the words, *body of Christ*. I placed the wafer in my mouth and whispered a prayer of thanksgiving as it dissolved in my mouth. Then came the cup.

Later, my husband took delight in telling how, at that moment, he could feel my rising tension. He attributed it to the fact that I was raised in the Deep South and that the couple just before me on the kneeler was African American. That wasn't the problem. It was the cup. THE cup—one.

I was used to having my own, tiny, sanitized, personal cup. I wasn't used to sharing. We didn't share at home, and we didn't share at church. Growing up, I drank out of the jelly glass with the cartoon characters on it, and my brother drank out of the glass mug that came with peanut butter in it. Mom and Dad had more grown-up glasses, but they each had their own, and nobody drank after anybody else. Even at family gatherings where chaos reigned, nobody shared. There was always a pen available so I could put my name on my plastic glass to insure its safety.

However, here in church, there was only ONE cup. I watched in dismay as the priest held the cup to the lips of each parishioner, then wiped the rim with a white linen cloth and turned the cup slightly so the next parishioner wouldn't drink from exactly the same spot as the last one. As if that would protect us from viruses and germs and other deadly microorganisms! Nevertheless, I remembered where I was and why, I sipped the wine, and I learned more about the community of Communion.

After a year or so, my husband started attending church less and less until I was finally attending alone, so I returned to the Baptist church. Christian seemed to enjoy church, especially the music and going to the donut shop beforehand, so he went with me. Still, he always had questions about Communion. Baptists practice closed Communion. When I was growing up in the buckle of the Bible belt, that meant you had to be a Baptist to participate. With time, the old ways relaxed a bit, but the preference was still that a person be a believer before he participated. Inevitably, this always led to the *why can't I have some* questions from the younger children, and I tried to use these as teaching moments. The results of those teaching moments and all the moments in Sunday school and church became apparent one morning on the way home from a service that had included Communion.

"Next time we have Communion, I'm going to take it," Christian announced as he played with his handheld game.

"You are?" I answered, wondering where this came from. "What's going to be different next time?"

"While you were taking Communion, I asked Jesus to come into my heart, and He said I could."

It sounded right to me.

About twenty years later, Christian was living in Colorado with his wife and a son of his own. He and Amy had planted a new church in Pueblo and were having meetings in their home on Wednesday nights. David and I were there for a visit and were privileged to worship with them during one of their early services. Disciples and Baptists are brothers in more ways than one; after services, there was food. My grandson, Mattias, was at the crawling around and pulling up stage, and as people milled around and visited, he spotted the remains of Communion on the coffee table. With his eye on the tempting loaf of bread, he grabbed the edge of the table, stood, and stretched out his little hand toward the treat. I was just debating about how to distract him when Christian came up and knelt beside his son. While my narrow-minded side worried about the propriety of giving a baby Communion bread, Christian pinched off a small bit and put it into Mattias' waiting mouth.

"Remember," he whispered. "Jesus loves you very, very much."

Amen.

My time of remembrance came to a close as the deacons returned to the front and the pastor stood up to pray. My plans for dealing with Mom didn't work out as well as I had hoped. She ate and drank immediately, so when the time came for everyone to partake, she forgot that she had already done so. She looked alternately at Dad and me with sad, puppy-dog eyes, wondering why she hadn't been allowed to participate. However, before the pastor had made his closing remarks, the whole incident was forgotten, lost in a mass of plaque-encrusted nerve tangles.

One day, though, she'll get an invitation.

"Helen," Jesus will say, "Why don't you come home for supper."

She will sit at His table, surrounded by the loved ones who have already arrived. Then, as she eats the bread and drinks the wine, she will remember.

CHAPTER 11
Music, Jesus, and Alzheimer's

Ephesians 5:19 *Speaking to yourselves in psalms and hymns and spiritual songs, singing and making melody in your heart to the Lord.*

Mom couldn't read music, but she played the guitar and the piano by ear, and she had a beautiful singing voice. When they were young, she and her sister, Fay, sang duets in church, and for a while, Mom led the congregational singing when no one else was available. It must have taken an enormous amount of strength to overcome her natural shyness and insecurity to stand up in front of people to sing, but music and Jesus were important to her.

Mom told stories of Saturdays, after all the chores were done, when friends and family gathered for a night of music. She joined her uncles, who brought their guitars or fiddles, and she played until her fingers bled, singing long into the night as long as anyone was awake to sing with her. Unfortunately, somewhere along the line, her passion became buried under self-doubt, worry, and fear.

By the time I was old enough to remember, Mom no longer shared her musical talent in public. She participated when a group sang around the piano at family gatherings, and she joined in the congregational singing at church, but she no longer sang solos or duets with Aunt Fay or anyone else. Her guitar stayed in the closet and was only dragged out when I begged hard enough for her to play a song for me.

She played the piano more often than the guitar, and she usually played old hymns instead of honky-tonk or gospel tunes. I would sit on the bench beside her and sing along, and as I got older, she taught me to sing harmony. When I began taking piano lessons and spent more time practicing, she spent less time at the keyboard and soon gave that up, too.

Through the years, family gatherings were more likely to center around the TV than the piano, and she and Dad stayed home from church more, so she sang less. However, when they came to live with David and me, they went to church with us regularly, and once again, Mom and I sang side by side. She struggled with some of the contemporary choruses, but she remembered the old hymns.

The senior adult ministry at our church had a monthly luncheon. It always included some sort of entertainment, and once in a while, that entertainment was a hymn sing. The audience called out requests, and everybody sang along. It was one of Mom's favorite events. At one hymn sing, someone requested "What a Friend We Have in Jesus." It was one of "our" songs, one of the first songs we'd sung together. As we sang, our eyes met, and just for a moment, her eyes cleared and my mother was there, as she had been before Alzheimer's. It didn't last long. As the clarity faded from her eyes, she continued to sing, but I couldn't make a sound past the lump in my throat. A couple of years later, there was another hymn sing, but Mom didn't show up. Sure, she was physically present, and she sang along, but she stumbled over some of the words, and when our eyes met, there was no clarity.

Eventually, Mom and Dad left my home and moved into an assisted living facility near my brother. When I visited her, we spent a lot of time just sitting together, holding hands. One afternoon, we were in the common area, and one of the Gaither Gospel music shows was on the television. Without conscious thought, I started singing along, and Mom joined in. Her words were garbled and incoherent except when she came to the word "Jesus." There was no connection between us, but every time Jesus' name came up in a song, she smiled and sang out clearly and with conviction.

Mom loved music. Between music and the name of Jesus, Alzheimer's didn't stand a chance.

CHAPTER 12
Breakfast Adventures

1 Corinthians 10:31 *Whether therefore ye eat, or drink, or whatsoever ye do, do all to the glory of God.*

Eating out became quite an adventure as Mom and Dad's respective dementias took a firmer hold. When combined with anything else, such as a doctor's appointment, a simple outing became exhausting, at least for me. On the other hand, a trip to the lab for blood work followed by a stop for breakfast provided a lot of writing material.

One particular morning, a week before their six-month checkups with their primary care physician, Mom and Dad had an early appointment at the lab. Since they had to go in fasting, I planned to take them to breakfast afterward. I woke up early so I could be completely ready before going in to see if they were up. They usually slept pretty late, and that day was no exception, so I knocked on their door.

"Good morning," I said. "It's time to get up. You both have appointments to get lab work done this morning."

"OH-kay," said Dad in his little singsong morning voice, snuggling down a little further under the comforter.

"Huh?" Mom mumbled in confusion as she struggled to free herself from a tangle of sheet and blanket.

Since there would be no physical exam involved, I kept the hygiene regime simple—wet wipes, deodorant, fresh shirts, hair brush, toothbrush. Thirty minutes later, we were headed toward the door.

"Where we goin'?" Dad asked—again.

"To get lab work done," I said, holding Mom's hand as she stepped over the threshold onto the front porch. Once she was safely out, I let go and lagged back to lock the front door. When I caught up with her at the car, she was tugging unsuccessfully at the handle of the driver's door.

"It's locked," she said.

"I'll get it," I said. "You don't want to drive, do you?" asked the Sarcasm Gremlin that lived inside my head.

"Huh?" she asked, confused again.

"Here ya' go," I said, shoving the Gremlin back into his box and opening her door. "You sit back here."

"It's cold," Dad said.

It was around 70 degrees, but knowing how sensitive their thermostats were, I had grabbed jackets. I handed one of them to him, and while he put it on, I took his walker and put it in the trunk. The jacket was a welcome distraction. Even though we both knew he had neither the strength nor the balance to fold the walker and stow it, his macho pride forced him to try every time we went anywhere.

With Dad taken care of, I turned my attention back to Mom. I handed her a jacket and helped her put it on.

"Do you want me to stand up?" she asked.

"No," I said, slapping that Sarcasm Gremlin upside the head. "I just need you to lean forward a little bit." Then, I fastened her seatbelt, and we were off.

The other end of the trip was a little easier than I expected. Mom could still unfasten her seat belt most of the time and open the car door herself. In addition, Dad was slow enough that I could have the walker out and in front of him before he made it to a standing position. The waiting room was easier than normal, too. We only had to wait a little over ten minutes, and Mom never got into her "why are we here and why do we have to wait so long" routine. The tests themselves were also easy. The doctor had ordered blood work only—no urinalysis. Securing a urine sample may seem simple, and it was for Dad. However, as I mentioned earlier, Mom was a different story.

After the blood tests were finished, we returned to our assigned seats in the car with minimal confusion and headed for the Village Inn. Since I was outnumbered two to one, I didn't want to go where I had to order at a counter or go through a buffet line. I wanted to sit at a table, order our food, and have it brought to us. The Village Inn fit that bill, and it was Wednesday, which meant a free slice of pie for each of us. I pulled into a parking space close to the door and prayed for a nice, peaceful breakfast.

"What are we doing here?" Mom asked.

"Eating breakfast," I said.

Soon, everybody was out and headed in the right direction, but she was still confused.

"What are we doing here?" she asked again.

"Eating breakfast. Are you hungry?" I asked.

"Yes," she said. "I'm always hungry."

The hostess seated us in a nice booth by the window, and the waitress brought us coffee and water. Then, we faced our next hurdle—the menu. The waitress had opened the menus to breakfast, but Dad immediately flipped back to the lunch section. Mom ignored her menu completely and looked over Dad's shoulder. The Kids often asked me to order for them, but even when they didn't, I tried to simplify the process as much as possible.

"Look," I said, flipping Dad's menu back over to the breakfast section. "They have a "Pick Four" breakfast here. Why don't we order that?"

"That sounds good," Dad said.

"Yes, let's have that," Mom said, pointing at the pictures.

"Okay," I said. "But you have some decisions to make." For the next few minutes, I went through the menu with them. With some guidance and explanation, Dad chose two eggs over easy, patty sausage, cinnamon apples, and pancakes. Mom's choice was easy.

40

"I'll have what he's having." Something told me we should avoid the over easy eggs, but I didn't listen.

I quickly made my own selections, relayed our orders to the waitress, and sat back to enjoy my coffee. Mom carefully arranged her coffee, her water, and her utensils in front of her. Then, she looked at me expectantly.

"Now what?" she asked.

"Now we drink our coffee and wait for the waitress to bring our food," I said.

She craned her neck and peered toward the kitchen. She turned back to me with a scowl on her face.

"When are they going to bring it?" she asked.

"As soon as they get it cooked. It will be a few minutes."

The food came before she became too bored or too disgruntled, but when it appeared, she was a little dismayed at all the choices laid out in front of her. To deal with her mealtime confusion, she had adopted a "one thing at a time" method of eating. She tried the eggs first, but dealing with the slippery critters proved to be too much of a challenge, so she turned her attention to the sausage. She had a great deal more success with it, and while she ate, I dissected her eggs.

"That was quite a bit of work for you," she said, looking at me with admiration.

I smiled and turned my attention to my own breakfast which, by then, was tepid. For the next few minutes, I watched her chase slippery pieces of egg around her plate, trying to stab them with her fork. Sometimes, she succeeded with a little bit of an assist from her other hand, but more often, her prize slipped back to the plate, and she came up empty.

"Mom, try scooping the fork under the egg instead of stabbing it," I said.

That method worked for one bite, but she promptly forgot the procedure and went back to stabbing. I suggested she try her spoon, and that worked a little better. She was finally able to finish the eggs with a little help from my fork on the last couple of bites. I removed her plate to keep her from obsessively scraping up the remaining egg yolk residue and put her bowl of apples in front of her. She immediately attacked them with her fork with much the same result she'd had with the eggs.

Once I substituted the spoon again, the rest of her meal went well. She finished the apples with no trouble, and after I gave her fork back, she polished off the pancakes I had cut up for her. As she scraped up the last few syrup-soaked crumbs, she flashed me a self-satisfied smile.

"I did it!" she said.

While Mom played tag with her eggs and apples, Dad was having his own little breakfast adventure. His use of utensils had become a little unorthodox over the past couple of years, especially since his right hand was a little numb from a stroke, but he managed to do the job. He finished his eggs, sausage, and apples without incident, even though his approach was unusual. After the first few bites of his meal, he pulled the saucer of pancakes closer to him and began breaking off bite-size pieces of pancake with his fingers, using them to push the slippery eggs onto his fork and to sop up the egg yolk from his plate. When the eggs, sausage, and apples were gone, he still had a pancake and a half left on his saucer. He pinched off another bite and stared at the plate with a kind of blank stare while he chewed. It was time for me to intervene.

"Here, Dad, let me make those a little easier to eat," I said, and I proceeded to slice and dice them like I did Mom's. He didn't object like he does sometimes when I offer to help. Maybe the struggle with the eggs had worn him out.

After we finished eating, there was one more decision to make. What kind of pie did we want? I narrowed the choices to a workable number, and we ended up with apple, cherry, and French silk—to go, please.

Then, there was a final challenge—the check. Dad liked to treat, and I liked to be treated, but he didn't tip. If I had been carrying cash, it would have been easy to leave a few bucks on the table, but I've always been a plastic kind of gal, so as he struggled to get his credit card out of his wallet, I plotted. He laid his card on the table while he put his wallet back in his pocket, and I picked it up. I preceded him to the register, and the deed was done before he arrived.

"Dad, do you want me to sign the credit card receipt, or do you want to do it?" I asked.

"You can do it," he said. Challenge met and waitress tipped!

I got everybody back into the car and buckled in, and we headed for home. As I pulled into the driveway, Mom asked, "Is this where we get out?"

I slapped that sarcastic little gremlin one more time and said, "Yes, this is home."

She got out of the car and made it up the walk and through the door. "Do you want us to go sit down?"

"Yes. Why don't you go on back to your living room? The air conditioner is on, and it's warmer back there."

"Our living room?" she said in confusion.

"Yes, right back through there and to the left."

She went left and continued going left, U-turning into the kitchen.

"Mom, back that way, through that door."

"That door?"

"No. That's the door to the lanai." I took her by the shoulders and gently turned her toward the correct room. "Right in there. Go on over and sit down on the couch, and I'll turn on the TV."

Finally, their blood work was done, and they were settled on the couch, watching afternoon soaps. They had eaten a nice meal, which they probably didn't remember, and I was exhausted. I decided that next time, I'd have the three-martini breakfast.

CHAPTER 13
Smart Phones and Smart Decisions

Psalm 86:7 *In the day of my trouble I will call upon thee: for thou wilt answer me.*

David gave me my first smart phone for Christmas two years after Mom died, and for a while, it was a lot smarter than I was. I quickly gained ground, though, and before long, I was downloading apps, taking and sending pictures, tweeting, and mastering the other essentials of staying in touch in the modern world. Mom would have been fascinated.

When her Alzheimer's moved from the beginning stages to the more serious ones, Mom developed a love/hate relationship with the telephone. From the time I became a latch key kid in third grade until she began to lose her ability to communicate, she and I talked on the phone almost every day. However, as she became more symptomatic, these conversations became difficult for her. She worried that she was bothering me or that I was too busy to talk with her, and she had trouble following the conversations.

She was even more paranoid about talking with other people, so she rarely called anyone, and her phone rarely rang. Even so, she carried the handset with her everywhere she went like an electronic security blanket.

Then, the phone stalking began. Somehow, her phone number ended up on a call list for some kind of robotic autodialer. Several times a day, her phone would ring, but when she answered, no one was there. She would hear mechanical clicks and beeps but no voices. In her state of mind, she was convinced that a stalker was calling her with evil intentions. In retaliation, she talked, cajoled, yelled, pushed buttons, and even blew a whistle, all to no avail. Dad added caller ID to their service, but she insisted on answering the phone anyway, and her hysteria mounted as the calls continued. David finally intervened and entered their number on the "no call" list. The calls eventually stopped, and she went back to peacefully carrying her security handset around.

Later, when cell phones became common enough that she was aware of them, she expressed a desire for "one of those phones you carry around with you." I pointed out that she had one she carried around, but she wanted one she could take outside. I managed to distract her from that idea until she forgot about it. Based on her experience with the other modern devices with buttons to push, that was probably one of the smartest phone-related decisions I ever made.

SECTION III
From Caregiving to Assisted Living

CHAPTER 14
The Traveling Years

Psalm 121:8 *The Lord shall preserve thy going out and thy coming in from this time forth, and even for evermore.*

Everyone feels like leaving home from time to time, especially caregivers. Before Mom and Dad moved in with us, it was easy for David and me to run away. We simply packed a few things in our saddle bags, climbed on our motorcycles, and took off. In the year before we became a four-person household, David put 40,000 miles on his bike, and I put 25,000 on mine. Then, I totaled my bike, we were transferred to Florida, and we became full-time caregivers.

During the next two years, our careers and settling into a new home and a new lifestyle occupied so much of our time there was little time to think about running away. Then, the economy forced both of us into early retirement, and the lure of the open road began to call us again.

There wasn't room for the four of us on David's motorcycle, but an RV had plenty of room for all of us, and it included all the comforts of home. We bought a forty-foot motor home, and, after a few test runs to local parks and campgrounds, we embarked on a seven-week, sixteen-state trek across the southeastern United States. We experienced enough adventures to fill a book, and many of them were enjoyable enough to make us fall in love with the RV lifestyle.

We ran away in our little home away from home as often as possible after that, sometimes taking Mom and Dad with us, and sometimes leaving them in the care of respite caregivers. Mom and Dad enjoyed our excursions, but each trip became more difficult for them and for us. I didn't realize just how difficult the trips had become until the following year when we arranged for them to stay with my brother while we took David's mom with us to Oregon to visit her sister. Then, we brought both of them back with us on the return trip. The contrast in traveling companions was amazing. While Mom and Dad were almost completely dependent on me, Betty and Jerry were not only independent but were also very helpful. The experience was very restorative, but it also made me realize how really stressful my caregiving role had become.

A year later, we took another long trip, this time with just the two of us. Once again, my brother hosted Mom and Dad while David and I traveled to Colorado for the birth of our granddaughter. After we celebrated her arrival and visited for a week or so, we drove down to Texas to take care of a real estate crisis.

We had learned that David's former roommate and current renter had abandoned the mobile home David had lived in before we married. While the management of the mobile home park had allowed the original renter to stay because of the situation, they would not let us rent to anyone new. We intended to purchase a small plot of land and move the home onto it. Our plan was to lease it for the short term and, depending on how that worked out, decide later what to do with it.

Land on the north side of Dallas proved to be out of our price range, so we moved east where we found the perfect place for us—two and a third acres with eighty-five trees and a tiny creek bordering the back of the lot. We spent the next few weeks supervising the move of the house, hooking up utilities, painting, cleaning, and otherwise preparing what we hoped would be the perfect rental property. The ad we ran in the local paper yielded quick results, and we headed back to Florida with a security deposit, first month's rent, and signed lease in hand.

That was the last of our long RV trips until we moved back to Texas, but the dream of one day going on the road again sustained us through the difficult days. Respite from the stress of caregiving is crucial, but when you can't get away, dreams of the next time offer hope.

CHAPTER 15
The Least of These

Matthew 25:40 *And the King shall answer and say unto them, Verily I say unto you, Inasmuch as ye have done it unto one of the least of these my brethren, ye have done it unto me.*

I wrote earlier about the unpleasant odors that sometimes result from the deteriorating hygiene practices of the elderly. One of these odors in our home emanated from the area around Mom's feet. I washed the tennis shoes she always wore and made sure she had plenty of clean socks, but it wasn't until I became more actively involved in her personal hygiene that I discovered the source of the smell.

Mom and I were alike in lots of ways, but wearing shoes was not one of them. I kick mine off as soon as I walk in the door and don't put them on until I'm walking out again or until the temperature dips close to the freezing mark. Mom, on the other hand, never bared a toe unless she was going to bed or taking a bath. When she and Dad first came to live with us, I never saw her feet because she was still going to bed and taking a bath on her own, sort of.

"Mom, it's time for you to take a shower."

"I don't want to."

"I know, but you need to anyway."

"Why? I just took a shower."

"It's been several days, and tomorrow's Sunday. You want to wash your hair and get ready for church, don't you?"

"I'll do it in the morning."

After a few more rounds of verbal sparring, she would give in and head for the bathroom, usually with Dad in tow. They would emerge an hour or so later sporting fresh clothes and combed hair but often smelling no better than when they went in. I began supervising her showers when we went on our first long RV trip, but it wasn't until I became a hands-on participant that I noticed her feet. That was when I discovered the source of the smell—her toenails.

I don't know how long it had been since her toenails had been trimmed, but they had grown out and over the ends of her toes. Several were thick and yellow and fragrant. I was shocked and shamed. How could I let this happen to my mom? I told myself I couldn't have known, but caregivers always feel responsible and guilty. I grabbed the toenail clippers and went to work.

It took several sessions to get the nails cut back to a reasonable length, but with regular trims, healthy nails eventually replaced the infected ones, and the foot odor disappeared. As I added another job to my growing list, I thought of something my aunt, who was a caregiver for many years, had said about the elderly.

People say caring for the elderly is like raising kids, but it's really not. Old people aren't cute, and they know less all the time instead of more. Sometimes, they smell bad, and they're hard to get along with, and people don't want to be around them. I think Jesus was talking about the elderly when He talked about the least of these.

It wasn't my favorite job, but as I sat on the floor at Mom's feet, I often thought of Jesus with a towel wrapped around His waist, kneeling at the feet of His disciples. I also thought about Mom's life that was getting smaller all the time. If her toenails needed to be clipped, it was the least I could do.

CHAPTER 16
Mom's Beautiful Curls

1 Corinthians 11:15 *But if a woman have long hair, it is a glory to her.*

Curls were always important to Mom. She often recounted the childhood heartbreak of having a plain, straight, Buster-Brown haircut while her sisters had curls and waves. She spent a lot of time and money chasing those elusive curls. With practice and persistence, she developed enough expertise with perm rods and pin curls to produce an acceptable result, but I came along to offer another challenge.

I was born with thick, black, curly hair, but before I reached my first birthday, it fell out and was replaced by white-blonde, straight locks. Mom knew exactly what to do. She gave me my first perm while I was sitting in my high chair. It took her so long to wind all the hair around the slim plastic rods that I fell asleep with my head on the tray. She must have thought the results were worth the effort because she continued to perm my hair every six months for years.

Between perms, she used pin curls to tame the fuzzy results of the harsh chemicals. Saturday afternoon was salon time around our house as we prepared for church the next day. She washed my long, thick hair and wound it up into tight little coils and hoped it would dry by morning. This was before affordable home dryers, and I spent many Sunday mornings standing in front of the heater, trying to remove the last of the dampness from my hair.

During the week, she woke me up early so she could fix my hair before she left for work. I was something of a tomboy, and she didn't trust me to make myself presentable on my own. If there was sufficient curl left from Sunday, she left it down, but most days she pulled it up into a pony tail. Sometimes, she put finger waves on the side and spit curls in the front. She was thrilled when she discovered a hairspray that made her creations last a little bit longer.

As I outgrew my tomboy phase and approached my teens, I took over maintenance of my own hair. She probably mourned the loss of my curls as I pursued the more straight-lined styles of the 60s, but she found lots to do with her own hair. New products and appliances came on the market on a regular basis, and she had enough toys to keep her busy. She ran through the gamut—pin curls, brush rollers, spoolies, magnetic rollers, hot rollers, and finally, curling irons and blow dryers.

When her memory began to fade, she still remembered how to take care of her hair. While she and Dad were still living on their own, it took her most of the morning to get through her beauty routine. I visited them regularly on my lunch hour, and she often greeted me with a hug and a smile—and hot rollers in her hair. By the time they moved in with us, she had abandoned the rollers in favor of a curling iron. She managed a nice-looking hairdo, but when her hair began to look really dry and brittle, I did some investigating. While she still curled her hair almost daily, she didn't wash it very often. She no longer used the hairspray, but she had a really heavy hand with the hairspray. She applied the hot iron to each strand and held it until it smoked, cooking the spray residue into a sticky mess that was destroying her hair.

In one of those role reversals that happen between children and parents as the years take their toll, I took over the role she had played in my life so many years before and began fixing her hair. She accepted the change easily. Her hands were twisted with arthritis, and using the curling iron had become painful as well as awkward.

There was a learning curve for both of us, though. Initially, I styled her hair with thin bangs swept slightly to one side. That was a mistake. After I finished and sent her back to her sitting room to watch TV with Dad, she would disappear into her bedroom and emerge a few minutes later with the curl completely brushed away.

Her hair would be parted on the side with her bangs secured firmly to the side with a bobby pin. After a few weeks, we both adjusted. I began to style the front of her hair into a soft wave that swept to one side, safely off her forehead, and she left it alone, especially after I hid all the bobby pins.

She came to love the special attention of having me fool with her hair. After her shower, I sat her on my vanity stool while I dried and curled and styled. She closed her eyes and relaxed, and if she had been a cat, I'm sure she would have purred. It was a sweet time for me, a time when I could show in a physical way how special she was to me.

As she got worse, the beauty sessions often confused her. While I worked, she sometimes told me how much she appreciated my help while Linda was busy. At other times, she worried she didn't have any money to pay me but told me that Elmer would pay me when he picked her up. I reassured her that it was my pleasure, and it was. All the payment I needed was the smile on her face when she looked in the mirror and said, "I look pretty good, don't I?"

When she moved into assisted living, I worried about who would fix her hair. In the first few pictures I saw after the move, her hair was parted on the side and combed flat against her head, almost like the Buster-Brown hairstyle of her childhood. I talked to my brother, and he found that the facility had an on-site salon. He set up a weekly appointment for her, so at least once a week, she had her hair done. She had Alzheimer's, but she was still a woman, and curls were still important to her.

CHAPTER 17
Makeup and Alzheimer's Don't Mix

Ecclesiastes 3:11 *He hath made every thing beautiful in his time.*

Mom worried with more than just her hair—she also worried about her complexion. She thought her coloring was uneven and her pores were too big, and she worried that every laugh line would turn into a huge wrinkle. She spent hours at the cosmetic counter, looking for the perfect product to keep her young and beautiful. She always used moisturizer, and she never went to bed without removing her makeup and applying her most recently purchased night cream. Like everything else in her life, Alzheimer's changed that, too.

Mom always wanted to put her best face forward, so she rarely went out of the house without applying makeup. Like everything else in her life, though, handling tubes and bottles and brushes became confusing and increasingly difficult. Before long, makeup was saved for special occasions, and eventually, she only wore it on Sundays. Her hands were unsteady, so I checked her for smudged eye shadow and smeared lipstick before we left the house, and I sometimes had to tone down her blusher a bit. She complained that she had rough spots on her cheeks, and she thought a little more color would cover them up.

One constant when dealing with Alzheimer's is that the situation will get worse, and this was no exception. One Sunday morning, the usual getting ready noises were absent from their side of the house, so I went to check on Mom and Dad. They were sitting on the couch in their sitting room, dressed in their jeans, staring at the blank screen of the TV.

"You're not ready!" I said, stating the obvious. "It's Sunday, and it's almost time to leave for church."

"We're not going," Dad said.

"I can't go looking like this," said Mom, pointing to her face.

I looked more closely and realized that the huge red splotches on her cheeks were not the result of an over-ambitious application of blush. Instead, they were raw, oozing patches that looked like the top layer of skin had been removed with sandpaper.

"What happened?" I asked in horror.

"I don't know," she said. "It just happened."

I went into her bathroom to get some ointment or something to sooth what had to be painful abrasions, and I saw several bloody tissues in the trash can. Apparently, she had decided to take aggressive action against those rough spots—and the results were disastrous.

Seeing how much trouble she was having putting the makeup on, I should have realized she would have at least as much trouble taking it off, but denial is strong, even in the face of the strongest evidence. By the time her face healed, I was doing more than simply prompting her through her bath routine; I was taking an active role.

One of the first things I noticed was that she didn't wash her face in the shower. I assumed that was because she was using special facial cleanser rather than regular body soap—at least she always did in the pre-Alzheimer's days. More investigation showed this was not the case, so I added face cleansing to our post-shower routine.

I paid special attention to her cheeks, which were healed but showed some faint scarring. I also paid attention to her forehead. During her last visit with her dermatologist, the doctor had commented on a scaly condition that had developed close to Mom's hairline. She used an unpronounceable medical term that basically meant some kind of psoriasis. She said it wasn't serious, and she'd look at it more closely at Mom's next checkup. I didn't wait, though, and I looked at Mom's forehead very closely as I cleaned and moisturized her face.

What I saw wasn't some kind of medical condition. What I saw was a buildup of makeup where Mom had failed to remove yesterday's cosmetics before applying more. Not wanting to make the same mistake Mom did on her cheeks, I cleansed gently and patiently, and over the course of a couple of weeks, healthy skin reappeared.

Mom still liked to look pretty, so I became her makeup artist. I worked on the less-is-more principal, using a tinted moisturizer in place of the thick liquid she had been using, and I used a very light hand with blush. I skipped the eyeliner and mascara, because she had trouble holding still when she saw me coming at her with a brush or a wand, but she was okay with closing her eyes while I brushed on a little shadow. I finished with a light lipstick that wasn't too obvious when it smeared. The result was clean and fresh, and it made Mom feel as pretty as she looked. Sadly, she would forget how pretty she looked as soon as she turned away from the mirror. If only I could have worked the same artistry on her fading mind.

CHAPTER 18
Mom's Busy Hands

Ecclesiastes 9:10 *Whatsoever thy hand findeth to do, do it with thy might.*

Writers are always up for a challenge, both issuing and accepting them. A friend once issued a challenge for her fellow writers to introduce someone simply by describing their hands. I immediately thought of Mom's hands. In an effort to describe them in one word, I thought of the word "busy."

I have always felt a bit of inward rebellion when someone talks about a "Proverbs 31 woman." The woman described in that chapter is too good to be true, like the superwomen described in magazines displayed at the supermarket checkouts. I can't relate to anyone who can hold down a full-time job, keep a perfect house, serve perfect meals, raise perfect children, and still have the energy to fulfill all her husband's fantasies. However, while the overall description may be overwhelming, the individual characteristics described in the chapter are less intimidating. Proverbs 31:13 says "She…works with eager hands," and that was a pretty good description of Mom's hands. She was probably taught that idle hands are the devil's workshop, and she took that teaching to heart.

Mom kept an immaculate house. At least once a week, everything from floor to ceiling and everywhere in between was swept, vacuumed, washed, or polished. Curtains and blinds were regularly taken down and washed, silver was polished, and spiders didn't dare start a web in one of her corners. She took a part-time job when I started first grade, but she was fast with a broom and still kept up with her cleaning. A few years later, when she went to work full time, she didn't lower her standards but, instead, enlisted the rest of the family to help in the weekly ritual—most of the family anyway. By then, my brother Jim was involved with school and church activities and various part-time jobs that exempted him, but Dad and I knew what our Saturday-morning duties were. I changed bed and bath linens, cleaned the bathroom, and dusted; Dad did the floors; and Mom stayed in the kitchen. She cooked a lot, especially on Saturday, and while she cooked, she cleaned. Her appliances always sparkled like they had just been delivered, and her kitchen floor really was clean enough to serve as a dinner plate if you were so inclined.

Her hands were fast as well as busy, so after she finished cooking and cleaning, she had time to spare. She filled that time with crocheting and sewing. She made lots of lacy white doilies for various table surfaces and chair arms. These were washed, starched, and ironed along with the rest of the laundry. As I got older, she took more interest in sewing. She made a lot of my clothes, and when she wasn't making something new, she was altering or repurposing something old.

When I got married and became the mistress of my own household, I found it hard to live up to her standards. My hands were much slower than hers, and I was more interested in socializing than she was, so I resented the time I spent cleaning. I wasn't as good with a needle as she was, either. I tried but could never get anything to fit just right, and I hated to redo anything. There was one thing we both enjoyed doing with our hands, though, and that was making music.

Mom never took lessons, but she loved music. In addition to guitar and piano, she could probably have played other instruments if she'd had access to them. I loved sitting in front of her and watching her hands on the frets and strings or sitting beside her and watching her hands on the keyboard. When I started playing the piano, I think she enjoyed watching my hands, too. She wasn't a touchy-feely kind of mom, but one Sunday morning, she was holding my hand during church. She laid my hand out flat on her lap and traced my fingers with hers.

61

"You have the long fingers of a pianist," she said.

In her later years, she hated it when her hands started to age. She bought jar after jar of vanishing cream to fight the brown spots that marred them, and she became self-conscious as arthritis twisted her fingers into painful knots. She held up her hands to family members and joked about being able to point to one side or the other without moving her hands, but in public, she kept them folded inconspicuously in her lap.

With the onset of Alzheimer's, her lifetime cleaning habits suffered along with other aspects of her life, but her hands remained busy. Many times, I saw her rooting around in her purse or a drawer, taking things out, examining them, and putting them back in. My theory was that she started looking for something but forgot what she was after, so she kept rooting around, hoping it would come back to her.

After she became unable to read, she didn't know what to do with her hands while she and Dad watched TV, so she picked. If she found a loose thread, she pulled at it until she unraveled a hem, or if she found a rough spot on her arm or her face, she scratched and picked it raw. If she found a stiff hair on her chin, she tried to tweeze it with her fingernails until the surrounding skin was red and angry looking, and she couldn't keep her hands off her teeth. She had some bone loss around the roots of her lower front teeth causing them to loosen. After she moved into a residential care facility where she no longer had me constantly reminding her to leave them alone, she worried two of them right out of her mouth.

In the last months of her life, Mom developed skin problems, and her hands got her into more trouble. At first, the doctors thought her outbreaks were caused by shingles, but they turned out to be a rare kind of autoimmune skin disease. The rash and the blisters were a constant source of irritation to her, so she scratched. Her caregivers finally had to encase her hands in protective mittens to keep her from causing further damage to herself. It was hard to hold her hands when she was wearing her mittens, but unlike her, I'm very touchy-feely, so I found a way. As her recognition of me faded, it was one of the few ways left of connecting with her. On one of my last visits, she didn't have the mittens on, and I was able to hold her hands skin to skin. The arthritis prevented me from laying them out flat like she did mine in church that day, but it didn't prevent me from remembering, and it didn't stop me from thanking God for her busy hands.

CHAPTER 19
Mom's Red Hat

Proverbs 17:22 *A merry heart doeth good like a medicine.*

My membership in the Red Hat Society was short but sweet. I never thought much about it except, like the lady in an old commercial used to say, "That's for some old person, not me!" Then, I discovered that Red Hat ladies may have some years under their belts, but they're definitely not old.

During our six years in Florida, we lived in a subdivision that offered lots of amenities, including some very nice walking paths. David and I were more active then, and since we both worked at home, we needed an excuse to get out of the house every day. We got up early, and after a quick breakfast and a perfunctory scan of the newspaper, we went for a walk. It was not only good exercise, but it was also a great way to meet our neighbors. We met Bill and Mary and became great friends with them, and I was invited to join a ladies' Bible study group. We also met two Red Hat ladies. I can still picture their faces, but I can't remember their names, which probably means that I'm closer to that "old person" in the commercial than I care to admit. For the purpose of this story, I'll call them Jean and Diana.

Jean and Diana were definitely not old. They were lively and friendly, always ready with a smile and a wave. They lived in the other end of the subdivision, so some mornings, we greeted each other as we passed in opposite directions, but sometimes, we caught them as they headed back home, and we walked together for a while. We exchanged pleasantries about the weather and our respective families, and they always asked about Mom and Dad. Everybody knew Mom and Dad because they saw me walking with them down to the corner and back on those days when I could get them off the couch. We also talked about community activities, and they told me about the Red Hat group that met in our clubhouse once a month.

I was surprised to find out that Jean was a member. She didn't look old enough. I learned, however, that younger women can join the group, but they wear pink hats until they reach the age of fifty. I also found out that the ladies not only had fun together but also did a lot of charity work. The more I heard, the more interested I became. When they invited me to come to a meeting, I thought, *sure, why not.*

"Bring your mom, too. She'd love it, and everyone would love her."

"Okay, we'll come. I guess I need to go hat shopping."

"Don't worry about that," said Diana. "I have lots. I'll bring a couple of extras to the meeting. You can get your own if you decide to join."

The next meeting was the Thanksgiving lunch. It was a wonderful meal, and the ladies collected a lot of food for a needy family. Mom enjoyed the food and the attention, but she wasn't sure about the hat. I signed us up, paid our five-dollar dues, and thanked Jean and Diana for the invitation.

We missed the December meeting because of scheduling conflicts, but our new venture gave me ideas for Christmas gifts. Mom was getting to the stage where she didn't really need anything, but now she needed a red hat, and so did I. I found a matching pair that would suffice without breaking the budget, and I went to the craft store. In addition to their red hats, these fun ladies also wear purple, so I bought some wide ribbon with purple flowers for hat bands and a couple of purple plumes for panache. We laughed and had fun on Christmas morning, but Mom never really liked her hat.

We went to the January meeting, and she fidgeted and complained about her hat until I finally told her it was okay to take it off. The February meeting was a luncheon at a local Japanese restaurant. By then, Mom was becoming more insecure and clingy and didn't want to go anywhere without Dad. I talked with the powers that be in the group, and they agreed it would be fine for Dad to come along for lunch. They said he could be our mascot, even without a red hat. The outing went fine, but the male presence disrupted the chemistry of the group. Shortly after that, Mom and I hung up our red hats. I could have continued without her, but her insecurities made it difficult for me to leave her, and I wanted to share any moments of respite with David.

One of the red hats came out of retirement once more before it went to the Salvation Army during our move to Texas. On one of his birthdays, I sent my son, Christian, a birthday card with a picture of a cat dressed in a cowboy hat and bandana. I got an e-mail thanking me for the card and commenting that he'd like to see David dressed up like that. None of us had a cowboy hat, but bikers always have bandanas, and I had a hat and a camera. David may not qualify as a Red Hat lady, but he's definitely a good sport. The resulting photo provided some welcome comic relief to a life that had become anything but comical.

CHAPTER 20
Who Are You?

Psalm 34:18 The LORD is nigh unto them that are of a broken heart.

A caregiver friend once confided in me that one of the hardest parts of her job was not knowing who would greet her when she woke up each the morning. Would it be the confident man she had known for half a century who could efficiently take charge of any situation? Or would it be the man who was struggling with a life-threatening illness, the one whose mind was so fogged by pain and medications he couldn't remember how to tie his shoes?

"Linda, sometimes, he will be fine for weeks on end, and then one day, he's out of it. Some days, he changes from hour to hour. I never know when we start a conversation which one I'm talking to, and it's really stressful."

I listened and nodded. I understood. The slide into dementia isn't a steady descent into forgetfulness but rather a two-steps-forward-and-one-step-back journey with detours and switch backs along the way. Dad knew exactly where to find a copy of every tax return he had ever filed, but the next day or the next hour, he didn't remember how to fill out a check. Mom might be able to set the table perfectly, or she might not be able to figure out how many forks were needed for four people. As my friend said, it was stressful and caused all kinds of guilt and anxiety if I reacted to one personality when the other was actually present.

As hard as these identity shifts were on me, I sometimes wondered what the situation looked like from the other side of the relationship. Dad seemed to recognize most people up until the end, but Mom's grasp on who was who was more tentative. She often forgot names even when she recognized faces, and she covered her lapses with a giggle, a lighthearted *Now who are you,* and a tone of voice that said *I'm just kidding.* As she got worse, she knew who Linda was, but she didn't always know I was Linda.

"I appreciate you helping me with my shower," she would say. "Linda usually does it, but she's just so busy."

When she moved into assisted living, she called all the blonde staff members Linda. I guess she was looking for a younger, cuter, less gray version of me. As unsettling as it was not to know which version of Mom would appear, it must have been terrifying to have someone she didn't recognize change her clothes or give her a bath.

I remember hearing a story about Ronald Reagan when he was in the final stages of Alzheimer's. After a visit from his son, he said this to one of the staff members:

"I don't know who that man is, but he always gives me a hug."

Caregiving is heartbreaking. There is sorrow and fear and frustration, and sometimes, neither of you knows who is whom. Still, in the end, there is love and there are hugs.

CHAPTER 21
Ouch! My Halo Is Too Tight!

Romans 8:1 *There is therefore now no condemnation to them which are in Christ Jesus, who walk not after the flesh, but after the Spirit.*

As a caregiver, I was told I was an angel, a saint, the most wonderful daughter in the world. I didn't feel like an angel or a saint, and there were times when I felt anything but wonderful. The longer I served as a caregiver, the tighter the halo got and the less appropriate the labels seemed.

One of the things I lost when Mom and Dad moved in with us was personal space. I'm a rather private person, and I need a certain amount of "me" time to be happy. On the other hand, as Mom's Alzheimer's progressed, being alone frightened her. Before they moved in with us, she drew security from Dad and his constant presence, but as his dementia made him less reliable, she transferred her dependence to me. If I was out of her sight, she came looking for me like a child looking for her mother. She lost her ability to focus on books or TV, so she was often bored and looked to me for entertainment, but she rarely wanted to follow my suggestions. Unlike me, she didn't enjoy being outdoors, so it was always too hot or too cold or too windy to take a walk. For a while, she enjoyed sitting on the lanai and watching the clouds or the birds, but after a while, she couldn't focus that far away from herself. If I coaxed her out to sit with me on the swing, she stared at me expectantly as if waiting for me tell her what we were doing and why. She continually searched for something to restore her sense of stability and order, and that was something I couldn't do. Her frustration became mine, and in my frustration, I avoided her.

Some of my avoidance was legitimate. For the first few years of our cohabitation, I continued my career, working out of a home office. I was often on the phone with a customer and couldn't stop to interact with her. Even when I was available, though, if she came prowling through the house, searching for me, I retreated behind my desk or the closed door of my bedroom. One day, I didn't move quickly enough, and she saw me disappear around the corner.

"Are you running away from me?" she asked. Her perceptive instincts lingered long after her logic fled.

"No, why would I do that?" I answered, as my halo tightened a little bit.

One of the reasons I avoided her was her desire to help. Any time she heard me in the kitchen, she poked her head into the room and said the words that affected me like fingernails on a blackboard.

"Can I help?"

When Christian was little, I loved having him sit on the counter while I cooked—stirring, tasting, and generally making a mess. It was fun, because even when he dropped eggshells in the cake batter, I knew he'd do better next time. It wasn't the same when Mom helped. She was a great cook before she was stricken, but Alzheimer's made simple tasks confusing, and she needed assistance with everything. When she helped, it took me twice as long as when I worked alone, and it was more than twice as stressful. More often than not, I put her off when she asked.

"Not right now, thanks. I'll let you know if I need help."

Her smile would fade in disappointment, and my halo would tighten a bit more.

Going to church on Sunday mornings became quite a challenge, too. At first, it was a matter of waking The Kids, reminding them that it was Sunday, and encouraging them to get up and get ready. As their minds deteriorated, the process required more of my involvement. Eventually, I got up an hour early so I could shower, dress, and eat before I woke them. They had their baths on Saturday, so we would go straight from bed to getting dressed. I would lay out Dad's clothes and help Mom, and I would finish my own last-minute touches like jewelry and lipstick while they had their morning cereal and coffee. After they finished, I would send Dad in to brush his teeth while I fixed Mom's hair and makeup, and, if all went smoothly, we would be out the door by 8:45. However, instead of going smoothly, this is how it usually went.

Dad didn't want to get up, and his razor didn't work right. Mom's drawers and closet had been mysteriously rearranged again, and I couldn't find her shoes. Coffee was spilled, and neither wanted to brush their teeth. Mom's purse had disappeared—again—and Dad didn't want to use his walker. Mom couldn't get her seat belt fastened, and Dad realized he hadn't shaved after all.

By the time we arrived at church, I was usually in anything but a worshipful mood. Since I was Super-Caregiver, it never occurred to me to ask for help as I wrangled The Kids out of the car and up the walk to the door. The trick was to get Dad's walker out of the trunk and around to his door before he tried to get too independent and fell, and to get Mom out on the other side where she was more than likely tangled in her seat belt. One morning, she managed to get unbuckled and out the door before I got the walker out of the trunk. She stood there in confusion, unable to remember if she was getting out or getting in.

"Mom, just close the door."

She looked at me as if I were speaking Swahili.

"Close it! Just get out and close it!!"

As my voice got louder and more strident, her eyes got wider, and she was unable to move. I rushed around, grabbed her by the hand, shut the door, and dragged her with me, grabbing the walker and reaching Dad just before he tried to step up on the curb unassisted. Summoning what little dignity I had left, I held Mom's hand and smiled at the sweet couple who greeted us at the door each

Sunday morning. He shook our hands warmly, and she hugged and fussed over us.

"There's my favorite family. You look beautiful as always, Helen. Are you taking care of this handsome man?"

Mom beamed and giggled with pleasure as she took Dad's arm, and the greeter turned to hug me.

"You are such a wonderful daughter," she whispered in my ear. "God bless you."

I wondered if she saw how impatient I'd been with Mom as my tarnished halo slipped down around my neck and threatened to choke me.

There were many other times of frustration, but there were more times of love and tenderness. I learned to relax when I could and forgive myself when I couldn't. I'd rather tell you about all the tender times and skip the others, but that wouldn't be fair. I wasn't an angel or a saint, and no other caregiver has to be, either.

CHAPTER 22
One Way to Deal with Caregiver Guilt

Philippians 4:7 *And the peace of God, which passeth all understanding, shall keep your hearts and minds through Christ Jesus.*

Sometimes, we have to stop and allow ourselves to realize we're doing a great job. As a dementia caregiver, I lived under a perpetual load of guilt. It was not true, rational guilt that came from wrongdoing but, rather, a constant vague feeling of unrest that continually ate at me. No matter how good a job I was doing, I never felt like I was doing enough. No matter how well I handled a situation, I always felt like I could have done better. Somewhere in the back of my mind, I had the unrealistic idea that if I did everything right, Mom and Dad would get better. When this didn't happen, when they continued to slip away from me, I wrestled with the feeling that they were losing the battle and that, somehow, it was my fault.

While facilitating the caregiver support group at my church, I discovered I was not alone in my struggle with guilt. Most of the members of the group dealt with the same issue. We knew that, for the most part, our feelings were unfounded, and we were doing the best job possible under the circumstances. We focused a lot of attention on encouraging each other and finding ways to overcome this guilt.

Too often, caregivers spend too much of their time dealing with perceived failures: Dad was angry today, Mom didn't want to eat today, my husband refused to take a shower today. Occasionally, they might talk or write about the good days—the laugh, the successful outing, the *I love you*—but those times are few and far between.

Certainly, we need to talk about the bad times—I would have exploded and burned out long before I did without the opportunity to vent. Nevertheless, I wonder how my attitude would have improved had I focused more on the positive. I kept a gratitude journal for a while. I bought a small spiral notebook, and each day, I wrote down at least three things for which I was thankful. Some days, the best I could do was to be grateful I had made it through the day. Thankfully, there were positive days when it was easy to come up with more than three things, and on the bad days, it helped to go back and remember.

My journal might have been more effective if I had added photos. If I had taken pictures of Mom and Dad when they were clean and groomed and smiling, it might have helped on the days when they were uncooperative and didn't smell so good. If I had taken a picture of Mom in her pretty pink nightgown when she had just said "Thank you for taking such good care of me," I might have been less frustrated when I had to mop the bathroom floor again because she didn't quite make it to the toilet. If I had made a note each time a doctor looked into my eyes and said, "You're doing a great job," I might not have felt like such a failure.

The Apostle Paul wrote about being thankful and focusing on the good things in his letter to the church at Philippi. Maybe he was thinking about caregivers, too.

Philippians 4:6–8 6 *Be careful for nothing; but in everything by prayer and supplication with thanksgiving let your requests be made known unto God. [7] And the peace of God, which passeth all understanding, shall keep your hearts and minds through Christ Jesus.*

[8] Finally, brethren, whatsoever things are true, whatsoever things are honest, whatsoever thing are just, whatsoever things are pure, whatsoever things are lovely, whatsoever things are of good report; if there be any virtue, and if there be any praise, think on these things.

CHAPTER 23
Jesus, the Caregiver

Hebrews 4:15 *For we have not an high priest which cannot be touched with the feeling of our infirmities; but was in all points tempted like as we are, yet without sin.*

Denial, anger, bargaining, depression, acceptance: all the classic stages of grief. As a caregiver, I would add another stage: burnout.

I denied there was a problem, and I was angry at Mom for changing before my eyes. I knew I was being illogical, unfair, and unloving, so the guilt added to the depression when it came. The doctors didn't help, the medications didn't help, and I continued to watch Mom slide down the slippery slope into forgetfulness. There wasn't a thing I could do about it, but my caregiving duties continued to increase. First, I made occasional visits, I checked to see that there was no spoiled food in the refrigerator, and I reminded her to change clothes. Next, I made daily visits, I prepared and served meals, and I laid out clean changes of clothes. Then, she came to live with me; I cut her food and reminded her which utensil to use and how to hold it, and I changed her clothes. I could no longer deny what was happening. I was still angry; bargaining didn't work, and I was in despair.

One afternoon, after a particularly trying morning, I sat in the swing on the lanai with my Bible, looking for solace. I came across the verse at the beginning of this chapter.

Yeah, I thought, but Jesus was never a caregiver!

"Oh really," said that Still Small Voice. "Are you sure?"

I thought about Joseph. We don't know a lot about him, and he's never mentioned after Jesus stayed behind in the temple when He was twelve. Some people think Joseph was quite a bit older than Mary and that he died before Jesus began His public ministry. If Joseph died from a lingering illness, Jesus, as the oldest son, may have helped Mary, especially with the more physical aspects of caregiving. He may have bathed Joseph even when he didn't want a bath. He may have insisted that Joseph use his cane even when he insisted he didn't need it. He may have stood by Joseph's bedside, holding his hand and comforting him as he breathed his last breath. As for Mary, one of the last things Jesus did before He died was to give over the care of His mother to His disciple John.

One of the greatest things about a caregivers' support group is knowing that you aren't alone, that there are others going through what you are , who know how you feel. Members empathize with and draw strength from each other. In those few moments on the lanai, I accepted the possibility that maybe Jesus had been a caregiver—that He really did know and understand what I was going through. I also accepted Philippians 4:13 which says, *"I can do all things through Christ which strengtheneth me."*

CHAPTER 24
Put On Your Own Oxygen Mask First

Luke 10:27 *And he answering said, Thou shalt love the Lord thy God with all thy heart, and with all thy soul, and with all thy strength, and with all thy mind; and thy neighbour as thyself.*

For most of us, becoming a caregiver is not in our life plan. It is not something we go to school for or train for. When I became a full-time caregiver, I had no idea of how to do it well or how to deal with the difficulties I encountered. I expected to find lots of help when we relocated to Florida where the population is decidedly on the gray side. I found a few sources, but the websites were confusing and hard to negotiate, and agencies were even more confusing and difficult.

What I really wanted was to sit with experienced caregivers who could tell me what to do. I talked with the counseling pastor at my church, and as often happens when you point out a need, he suggested that I start a group to fill the need I saw. The short version is that after much thought, prayer, and the agreement of another couple to partner with us, David and I became facilitators of a caregivers' support group.

For the next several weeks, we made plans and spread the word about the new group. As I talked with people about the need for caregiver support, I received many different reactions, but one reaction really surprised me. Some people were uncomfortable admitting that being a caregiver was a difficult task. A common response was, "Oh, we're doing great. Mom (or Dad, or Aunt Jane or Grandpa Joe) is wonderful, and I have help from my husband (sister, brother, cousin)."

However, as I talked about my own situation, I began to hear things like this:

"It's hard to go out to dinner or a movie or a party without her because I feel bad leaving her to eat alone."

"We have a running battle over the thermostat setting."

"Some days I can't seem to do anything right."

In addition, those who acknowledged that life as a caregiver was less than ideal resisted becoming involved in a support group. Somehow, they felt disloyal admitting they needed help in taking care of their loved ones.

One lady expressed it this way: "I went to a support group one time when Mother was still living with us, but I never went back. I felt like I was sneaking out on her."

Once we began having meetings, some caregivers had a hard time arranging their situations so they could attend. Others felt guilty for being there. As facilitators, we discovered that one of our primary jobs, at least initially, was encouraging our members to give themselves permission to take care of themselves. We developed an informal mission statement that said, *Put on your own oxygen mask first.*

Anyone who flies very often probably tunes out when the flight attendant makes the safety announcements. However, there is one announcement that is very important to caregivers. *In the unlikely event we experience a loss in cabin pressure, oxygen masks will drop down from the panel above you.* Passengers are instructed that, if they are flying with a child or someone who needs assistance, they should put their own mask on first and then help others. Why is this important? If a person tries to put someone else's mask on first and, in the process, passes out from lack of oxygen, both are in trouble.

I have heard stories of missionaries who work in extremely depressed areas where people are starving. In the ultimate act of altruism, the missionary starves to death after giving their food away. This sounds very noble, but after they're gone, who works with the outside agencies to bring in more food? Who tells them about the love of Jesus?

Some caregivers are like these missionaries. They give everything they have to the person they love to the point they have nothing left to give. The result is burnout, health problems, and worse. It's not uncommon for the caregiver to die first, simply because they fail to take care of themselves.

Believing in the principle is one thing, but learning how to care for oneself in the midst of caregiver chaos is another. Each caregiver has to find what works in their situation, but I have a few suggestions based on my experience.

First, arrange for some privacy. Two years before Mom and Dad moved in with us, Dad spent five weeks in the hospital with a mysterious neurological infection, and we had our first experience with caring for Mom in our home. She would wake up in the middle of the night after having a bad dream and barge into our bedroom, turn on the lights, and look for Dad. When I shared this with Aunt Fay, who cared for my grandmother for many years, she said, "Linda, it may sound mean, but get a lock for your bedroom door and use it."

A couple we knew in Texas took his mother into their home after his father died, and they used his mother's limited mobility to ensure some privacy. They sold both homes and bought something that suited their needs. It was a beautiful home, and when I was given the grand tour, she explained.

"Mom has her own bedroom and bathroom downstairs. The rest of the bedrooms are upstairs, and we also have a sitting area up there with a TV and stereo. We did that intentionally. Mom can't negotiate the stairs, and sometimes we need to get away." It was an arrangement that worked well for everyone.

Next, do some things just for you—take a bubble bath, read a good book, take a walk. David and I enjoyed walking together, but it was sometimes hard to find the time. However, we knew how important it was, so we made the time by setting the alarm thirty minutes early so we could walk before Mom and Dad woke up. We enjoyed the quiet time so much we even set the alarm on Saturday.

During the years I cared for Mom and Dad, I learned a lot more about caregiving, and I found a lot more sources for help. Wherever you find help, it's important to know you don't have to do it alone. It's vital that, as a caregiver, you give yourself permission to take care of yourself. As a caregiver, self-care is not selfish; it is essential.

CHAPTER 25
My Fading Health

Philippians 2:27 *For indeed he was sick nigh unto death: but God had mercy on him.*

In spite of the best self-care, the stress of caregiving can take its toll. I woke up in the wee hours one morning feeling really strange. A trip to the emergency room revealed that my heart was beating irregularly and my heart rate was almost two hundred beats a minute. Two days in the hospital and a battery of tests produced a diagnosis of lone atrial fibrillation with no cause other than stress. Thanks to regular visits with a cardiologist and a couple of new medications, my heart behaved itself at least well enough to avoid any more hospital visits. However, there was another problem.

For several years, my primary care doctor had been keeping an eye on my perpetually high white blood cell count. He finally became concerned enough that he sent me to a hematologist who confirmed that I have a form of leukemia called CLL or Chronic Lymphocytic Leukemia. That's not as dramatic as it sounds. It's an indolent form that has few symptoms and fewer treatments. Still, just to make sure there weren't any hidden symptoms, I was poked, dyed, scanned, and tested on a regular basis.

At one point, in order to be sure my spleen and other organs were not involved, I had a CT scan and some blood work that was complicated enough to make a crime scene tech sit up and take notice. The day before the procedures, I went to the lab and picked up two ounces of clear liquid that was to be mixed with a juice of my choice and taken in three installments beginning a couple of hours before the procedure. I should have suspected something when the contrast came in a specimen bottle. That stuff was so nasty that even raspberry lemonade didn't cover up the bitter taste, and regardless of what you see on TV, holding your nose while you drink it doesn't help.

To make matters worse, the lab tech threw down the at-your-age card. Because they planned to inject me with an intravenous contrast in addition to the oral version, and since I was at such an advanced age, I was instructed to arrive thirty minutes early so they could draw blood and test my kidney function.

Dutifully, I followed instructions, including drinking the prescribed eight ounces of yucky stuff at the prescribed intervals; I arrived at nine o'clock, ready to fill out paperwork and have my insides dyed and scanned. After a brief wait in the lobby and another in the lab, the lab tech efficiently and almost painlessly inserted a picc line in my arm, withdrew an ounce or two of my aging blood, and left. I assumed my kidneys were functional enough to withstand the coming ordeal, because after a while, another lady in a lab coat appeared at the door and told me to follow her.

She led me to a room that contained a large donut-shaped machine with a board sticking out of the hole. She told me to lie down on the board, which moved in and out of the donut while a disembodied voice told me when to hold my breath and when to breathe.

When the CT ride came to an end, I went to the hematologist's office to have more blood drawn. The procedure wasn't quite as efficient or painless as in the other office, but a vein in my hand finally gave up the five vials of blood that were needed, and I went home bandaged, bruised, and thoroughly tested.

The results of all the tests were good, showing no complications that required anything other than close monitoring. At least there were no medical complications. The complications came in scheduling. Now, in addition to Mom and Dad's primary care physician, neurologist, urologist, dermatologist, dentist, and eye doctor, I had to find time for my quarterly visits to the hematologist and semi-annual visits to the cardiologist. Regardless of the inconvenience, I made up my mind to follow doctors' orders exactly and to do everything I could to live a long and healthy life.

CHAPTER 26
I Can't Do This Anymore

Proverbs 17:17 *A friend loveth at all times, and a brother is born for adversity.*

Accepting the fact that you can no longer care for your loved ones without help is one of the hardest things a caregiver has to do. I remember vividly the moment when I realized I could no longer deny that fact.

It had been a long, trying weekend. Saturday, Dad fell in the shower with a thump that echoed through the house. Being sensitive to his modesty, I peeped through a small crack between the folding doors to see if he was moving. He was, so I called out.

"Dad, are you okay?"

"Yeah, I'm fine."

"Are you sure?"

"Yeah, I just can't get up."

"Do you want me to help, or do you want me to go get David?"

"No, I'll do it."

"Get on your hands and knees. You can get up easier from there."

I continued to watch as he followed my directions and struggled to his feet.

"I'm up," he said.

"Great. Are you okay? Do you think you broke anything?"

"Nothing's hurt. Just my pride."

I whispered a prayer of thanks and went back to drying Mom's hair, listening closely for any further catastrophes. When he emerged from the bathroom a few minutes later and settled into an easy chair in the living room, I breathed a sigh of relief.

Sunday morning, he was fine except for a little soreness from his fall, but Mom wasn't doing well. I had trouble waking her, and once she was conscious, she was incoherent. Since she was in the middle stages of Alzheimer's, confusion was normal, but this was way beyond normal. I helped her out of bed, but she moved very slowly, shuffling to the bathroom and leaning on me for balance. She didn't seem to be in pain, and she didn't have a fever, so we continued through our Sunday routine, making it to church and back without incident.

Monday morning, she was no better, so I called her doctor's office. It was after hours that evening before he returned my call. When I explained her symptoms, the doctor was concerned.

"It sounds like she has some kind of blood infection. You need to take her to the emergency room now."

So much for dinner plans. I gathered jackets, medication lists, and other necessities, and I herded Mom and Dad to the car.

"Do you want me to come with you?" David said.

"No," said Super Caregiver. Then, I uttered those famous last words, "I'll be fine."

I spent the next several hours explaining why we were there, reassuring Mom and Dad that the doctor would be with us soon, and holding Mom's hands so she wouldn't pull the IV out of her arm. She was finally diagnosed with a kidney infection, hydrated with intravenous fluids, pumped full of antibiotics, given a prescription, and released.

After a quick stop at the pharmacy, we arrived at home, and chaos ensued. Mom seemed a little steadier on her feet, but she was still wobbly. I supported her onto the porch and told her to hold on to Dad's walker. I turned to unlock the door, and she hit the cement.

"Mom, are you okay?"

She moaned in reply.

"Dad, get back."

"I'm going to help her up."

"Dad, let me do it. You'll fall, and I'll have two of you to deal with."

"I'm not going to fall."

"You just fell in the shower Saturday."

"I'm going to help her up."

Thank goodness for cell phones. Holding Dad at bay and comforting Mom, I grabbed mine and called David.

"We're on the front porch. Mom fell. Help!"

We helped her to her feet, kept Dad on his, and put them to bed without further incident. Mom was bruised but not broken. By morning, the medicine was working, and she was back to normal. I wasn't, though. After breakfast, I picked up the phone and called my brother.

"Jim," I said, "I can't do this anymore."

CHAPTER 27
Decision Time

Genesis 47:11 *And Joseph placed his father and his brethren, and gave them a possession in the land of Egypt, in the best of the land, in the land of Rameses.*

The next few months were almost as chaotic as the seven weeks we had spent in the RV several years earlier. While Jim checked out the assisted living options in Conway where he lived, David and I investigated our own options. After we both became unemployed, we got more serious about our stock trading, and we did well enough to keep our finances stable. However, the instability of the stock market had shown us we were not the astute traders we had imagined, and the cost of living in Florida continued to rise. We no longer needed the large house we had purchased to accommodate the four of us, and we had a smaller house that was soon to be vacant in Texas.

The plans we had made two years before to become landlords hadn't worked out well at all. The first renter paid two months of a twelve-month lease before moving out, taking the small amount of furniture we had left and all the appliances with them. The second lessees paid three months' rent, and then continued to live on the property rent free in spite of our long-distance attempts to correct the situation.

We loved our life in Florida, but our choice seemed obvious if not easy. Even as the cost of living rose, the real estate market had fallen steadily since we had bought our house. However, based on our previous landlord experience, we decided against trying to lease, and we put the Florida house on the market. Selling a home is always complicated, but owing more than the house will bring in the current market geometrically increases the complications. The bureaucratic red tape required for a short sale was enough to unnerve the most tranquil person, and at that point, I was far from tranquil.

Even though the decision had been made, I still struggled with the idea of moving Mom and Dad into assisted living. Then, one Sunday morning during the fellowship time before Bible study, a friend told me her story of making a similar decision.

"We cared for my father-in-law in our home for many years, but when the time came that he needed more care than we could give him, I struggled with the decision. One morning, I sat down with my Bible, searching for an answer. I came to the story in Genesis of when Joseph became the second in command in Egypt. Because of the extensive famine, he sent for his aging father so he could care for him. He didn't move his father into his home, though. Instead, he settled Jacob and the rest of his family in the land of Goshen. Caring for your parents in your home isn't the only way for you to honor them."

It was still a time filled with stressful decisions, but her words helped when the guilt threatened to become overwhelming.

CHAPTER 28
Confusion and Clarity

1 Corinthians 13:12 *For now we see through a glass, darkly.*

As the time drew closer for Mom and Dad to move, my anxiety increased. A few days before the big event, I went to Wal-Mart and became really choked up, almost to the point of hyperventilating. Maybe it was the package of adult diapers I picked up.

This is probably the last package of these I'll have to buy. I wonder how Mom will react to a stranger changing her underwear.

Maybe it was the vitamins I put in the basket for David and me.

I won't have to buy and sort Mom and Dad's medications any more. That will be the job of another stranger. What if they don't do it right? I hope they check to be sure Dad doesn't drop some of his pills on the floor and that they give Mom her pills a few at a time so she doesn't chew them. I'm not sure I can go through with this—but I'm sure I have to go through with it.

The day before my brother Jim arrived to begin the moving process, my son instant messaged me, asking how I felt about it.

"Are you feeling relieved, anxious, survivor's guilt?"

"Yes. All of the above."

In the hope of avoiding undue stress for everybody, and as a result of past experience, I had waited until the last minute to tell Mom and Dad of the impending changes. I told them what was happening at dinner that night. Dad listened attentively and said nothing. Mom listened and screwed up her face as if she was about to cry.

"But I don't want to go with Jim."

"It'll be fine, Mom. He's your son. You stayed with him in September when we went to Missouri, and you had a great time."

"I guess," she said. She wasn't convinced.

"You'll have a nice apartment close to Jim, and he'll come visit you and check on you."

"I have an apartment by Mama," she said.

"No, it's by Jim," I said without thinking.

"Mama!" she said.

"No, it's by Jim."

"MAMA!"

I'm slow, but I finally got the message and let it go. I sat for a few more minutes, waiting for more reaction. When none came, I began to breathe normally again, and I went into the kitchen to do the dishes. I felt a little guilty for not asking if they had questions or encouraging them to express their feelings, but the relief was strong, and it chased the guilt away.

Dad was oblivious and went about his usual task of putting away the place mats, but Mom was agitated. She watched me more closely than usual, and when she brought the glasses from the table to the counter, she hovered. When Dad finished his job, he headed for the wing chair to the left of the couch, and Mom followed his example, making her way to the overstuffed chair opposite him. Her butt couldn't have done more than brush the microfiber surface of the seat before she was standing in the kitchen again, drilling me with a purposeful stare. I sensed a bad session of sundowners coming on.

"What do you need?" I asked.

I can't possibly reproduce on paper the series of sounds that proceeded from her mouth as she struggled to convey her thoughts. Somewhere in the gibberish, I picked up on the word *pay* as she gestured toward the leftovers I was putting away, and I assumed she was dealing with a familiar concern.

"Are you worried about paying for your dinner?"

Her body language indicated I was on the right track.

"Don't worry about it," I said. "It's been taken care of."

Her look spoke volumes. *I wanted to do something nice by picking up the check. Why won't you let me?*

"Mom, you and Dad pay for half of the groceries, so you've already paid for it."

"I guess that works," she said in real words.

She returned to her chair, and I returned to the dishes. Silence fell over the room. The only sound was the tick of the timer on the table lamp and the occasional click of David's mouse—that and the nagging caregiver's guilt.

"Dad, did you have any questions about what's happening?"

"No, no questions."

The silence returned for a couple of minutes.

"I guess I do have one question," he said. "What's happening?"

I had waited until the last minute to tell them, because I knew they would either forget or worry, but I expected them to retain the information for more than ten minutes. After I explained again the changes that were coming, I finished the dishes, David went back to his computer, and Mom and Dad contemplated whatever random thoughts chased each other across their minds. When I finished, I joined the rest of the family in the living room and settled down to read.

"So, you and David are moving back to Texas," Dad said after a few minutes.

"Yes, eventually. But we're going to travel around the country for a while." We weren't really sure how much traveling we would be doing. Based on our experience as landlords, it was likely we would simply move into the Texas house ourselves. However, to avoid questions about why they couldn't move to Texas with us, I didn't mention that possibility.

"What are you going to do with your furniture?" he said.

"We'll put it in storage until we settle down."

That was all the questions. Nothing about how they would care for an apartment and themselves after years of living under my constant supervision. No worries about how their furniture would be moved and who would foot the bill for the move and the new apartment. With no further questions and no TV to distract them, the nightly ritual soon began. Mom did whatever a wife of almost seventy years does to catch the eye of her husband. Through mouthed words and various gestures, she communicated her message, and when she received the desired answer, she turned to me.

"I think we're going to bed," she said.

"Okay," I said, glancing up from my book.

"I guess that's okay with you."

"Sure," I said, too absorbed in my reading to catch the undertone at first, the one that said *You'll be glad to get rid of us.* As her unspoken message penetrated, I looked up with a reassuring smile.

"Come on. I'll help you put on your nightgown."

We went through the routine of undressing, slipping into a pink, satiny gown she insisted was too pretty to wear, and making one last visit to the bathroom. We hugged, kissed, and exchanged *I love yous.* Then, while she crawled under the covers, I went to the other side of the bed where Dad sat with his shirt unbuttoned, waiting for me to leave so he could finish undressing. We performed a more restrained version of the hug-kiss-love-you dance, and I turned out the overhead light, leaving them in the soft glow of the night light.

"I'll see you in the morning," I said.

"Okay," Dad said.

Mom raised up on one elbow, clutching the covers under her chin. "Because we won't hardly ever see you anymore," she said.

Sometimes, her moments of clarity were as heartbreaking as her moments of confusion.

CHAPTER 29
Parting Is Such Sweet Sorrow

Acts 13: 3 *And when they had fasted and prayed, and laid their hands on them, they sent them away.*

Jim arrived the next day. Mom and Dad were glad to see him and didn't give any indication they remembered what was coming. They didn't seem disturbed by the activity of moving furniture and boxes from their room to the small trailer we had rented. They were content to sit together on the couch in the family room and watch TV while the love seat and TV were moved out of their sitting area. The guest bed was in better shape than their bed, and it would fit into their new apartment more easily, so they hardly noticed when it was put in the trailer. When bedtime came, their bed was still in its place, so they were happy.

Jim's son, Sean, flew in a couples of days later so he could drive the truck and trailer back to Arkansas. He woke up early the next morning, planning to drive straight through so he could be back at work by Monday. Jim would follow with Mom and Dad at a slower pace, allowing plenty of time for rest stops and meals and spending at least one night on the road. He would be driving them in their beloved Buick Skylark.

The Buick was thirteen years old, and it was showing its age. The outside mirror adjustments had long ago come loose and fallen into the inner recesses of the doors. The glove compartment no longer stayed shut even with the help of duct tape. The carpets were stained from food spilled on the way to potluck dinners, and when the doors were first opened on hot Florida afternoons, the lingering odor of unwashed bodies and incontinent passengers drifted out into the sunshine. Nonetheless, to Mom and Dad, it was still as beautiful as the day they'd driven it off the lot, the day Dad's eyes filled with tears and he said, "I didn't think I'd ever own a Buick." They still smiled with pride when they looked at it, and one or the other would say, "That sure is a pretty car."

They felt the same way about each other. After seventy years of marriage, he looked at her like a starstruck teenager, seeing past the wear and tear of the years to the woman he loved and saying, "You're beautiful."

"And you're handsome," she would say with equal sincerity as they exchanged kisses and smiled into each other's eyes.

That morning, however, they weren't focused on each other or on the Buick. They were confused.

"Good morning," I said as I knocked on their door. "It's time to get up and get dressed."

"Why?" Dad said without moving.

"You're going to Arkansas today with Jim."

"We are? What for?"

Sighing silently, I went through the explanation—again. "We've sold the house, and we have to be out in about ten days. David and I will be living in the RV for a while, and it's not big enough for all of us. Besides, Jim wants you to live in Arkansas for a while so he can see you more often. He's found a nice apartment for you about two miles from his house."

I stopped myself from saying *Don't you remember?* Of course, they didn't remember. In spite of the repeated explanations and all the furniture they had seen being carried out of the house, they didn't remember. Alzheimer's and dementia saw to that.

When the time came for them to get in the car, Dad hugged and kissed me goodbye with little more emotion than if we were saying goodnight, but Mom teared up, fear clouding her face. "I don't want to go," she said.

"You'll be fine," I said. "You'll have a good time."

"Yeah," said Jim. "I'm a lot more fun than she is."

"Yes, he is," I said. "And he's not nearly as bossy."

Once they were in the car, neither of them looked back. I watched until they were out of sight and returned to the house to try and bring order to the chaos. Mom's last look haunted me, and the pain of their departure lingered, but it was tempered by the relief of not having them underfoot. We left the doors and windows open with no complaints about how cold it was. I sorted, boxed, bagged, and stacked without repeated questions about what I was doing and why. We also had some periods of comic relief when Jim emailed reports on how the trip was going.

His first report read like this: "Mom was fine as soon as we were out of the driveway, but Dad asked about a dozen times in the first two miles where Linda was."

The second was equally optimistic: "I don't know why I was worried about Mom and her bathroom needs. I just sent her into the restroom with a fresh Depends and she was fine."

I knew there would be a follow up to that one—and there was. It read: "Maybe she does need supervision after all. She apparently put the clean one on over the dirty one."

By the fourth update, reality was setting in: "Which suitcase is Dad's and which is Mom's? Dad needs a change of clothes."

The fifth update came the next day: "I planned to spend a night on the road. We stopped and got a motel room, but by 2:00 am when Mom was up AGAIN, I gave up, packed the car and headed for home."

Transitions are always hard, but all things considered, this one went amazingly well. When Mom and Dad walked into their new apartment where their furniture, pictures, and other personal belongings had been set up, they seemed to feel right at home.

"Oh," Dad said as he looked around. "Is this our place?"

We had a lot to do before we left for Texas: a garage sale to prepare for; closets, drawers, and cabinets to clean out; years of memories and stuff to be sorted, saved, donated, and discarded. There's always time, though, for the caregiver to doubt, to second guess, to worry, to regret, and to grieve.

CHAPTER 30
Being Grateful

1 Thessalonians 5:18 *In every thing give thanks.*

When I was going through my crisis, my attitude about everything really sucked. I had heard people talk about keeping a list of things for which they were thankful and how much it helped them, so I gave it a try.

I bought a small spiral notebook and made a commitment to make three entries a day. It was easy at first because I could write down the big things like Jesus, my husband, our nice home. However, as time went on, I tried not to repeat myself, so it became harder. Our lives became more stressful, and some days, all I could write was Thank You that this day is over. In the long run, though, it helped. Those few moments each day of focusing on the positives in my life helped me face the negatives with a better attitude.

After Mom and Dad left for Arkansas, while I was organizing and packing for our move, I came across that little notebook and read through a few entries. Some of them made me laugh as I remembered the situations that inspired them, but most of them were anything but laughable at the time.

Thank you…

…for dedicated doctors who continue to practice in spite of all the bureaucracy.

…for helping me through the tough times with Mom and Dad.

…for a wonderful six-hour break with David.

…for Depends.

…for the man at the medical supply who fixed Dad's walker for $18.

…for Brenda. (Brenda was a caregiver who came in once a week for a few hours.)

…that my blood pressure is finally down.

…that Dad took a bath without incident and even shaved!

…for Liquid Plum-R. (Dad frequently stopped up the toilet.)

…for a relatively smooth trip to the lab and to breakfast.

…that even with the time change and picking up refreshments for Sunday school, we made it to church on time.

…for the porch swing and the lanai.

…for easy house cleaning products.

…that Mom didn't choke on her food at dinner.

…for wisdom even though I don't always use it wisely.

…that we can still leave Mom and Dad alone from time to time.

…for unstopping the toilet.

…for David to lean on in this stressful time.

…that there is space available at Southridge Village for Mom and Dad.

…that Sean can help with the move.

…for the years I've had to take care of Mom and Dad.

The last item in that gratitude journal conveyed the huge sense of relief I was beginning to feel. It said simply and without apology, thank you that it's Jim's turn.

CHAPTER 31
My Dad, the Troublemaker

Acts 16:26 *And suddenly there was a great earthquake, so that the foundations of the prison were shaken: and immediately all the doors were opened.*

Dad was always a by-the-book kind of guy. As far as I know, he never had so much as a parking ticket, and the worst expletive I ever heard him say was *good honk.* That's why I was surprised when he and Mom moved into assisted living and he started causing trouble.

After the residents retired to their apartments each night, a staff member checked on them every couple of hours. When they tried to check on Mom and Dad the first night, they couldn't open the door. There were no locks, but Dad had wedged his four-legged cane under the door knob. The next night when he went to bed, they put his cane in a closet, but he pushed a chair against the door. He was pretty resourceful for an old guy with dementia. His paranoia was short-lived, though, and he soon gave up trying to bar the door.

Then, he started to wander. An hour or two after bed time, he was often seen, dressed in his PJs, wandering the halls. At first, the aides were afraid he was trying to make a break for it, but he couldn't walk very fast or very far, so they didn't worry too much. They kept an eye out for him, and when he took his nightly stroll, one of the aides met him in the hall and escorted him to the common area where there were couches and chairs. It was close to the staff work area, so they could listen for the phone or the intercom while they visited with Dad. He wasn't very lucid, and maybe not even fully awake, but they chatted with him until he was ready to go back to bed.

He must have mumbled something about sorting mail or postage, because after a few evenings of this, they realized he was talking about the post office. He had been employed by the postal service for twenty years, and for a large part of his career, he had worked nights. He slept on a split shift, napping for a few hours in the afternoon before the rest of the family returned home and catching another hour or two before going to work. Apparently, he was reverting to those days, waking up after a couple hours of sleep, ready to go sort some mail.

Because of his nightly wanderings, and because they needed more lockdown space anyway, locks were installed on the doors from Dad's wing into the rest of the facility. A keypad was installed, and a code was required to unlock the door. Since he couldn't remember the code even if someone gave it to him, Dad was free to wander at will. With both his paranoia and his wanderlust under control, Dad was off the bad boy list. Then, along came John.

John moved into an apartment at the opposite end of the hall where Mom and Dad lived. John was very confused and very vocal, and he was definitely a flight risk. He roamed the halls in his wheelchair, voicing his complaints in a loud and commanding voice.

"I don't know what I'm supposed to do."

"Can you open that door for me?"

"Where is my car?"

"How did I get here?"

"When is my daughter coming?"

One night, his roaming and Dad's wandering crossed paths, and John thought he had found an accomplice. The aide returned from doing a room check and found both of them in the common area. John was sitting behind the staff desk with his wallet open and a five-dollar bill in his hand. Dad was standing in front of the desk in his pajamas, listening attentively.

"I'll pay you to open that door for me," said John.

I'm not sure what happened to John, but after my first visit, I no longer saw him rolling through the hallways. As for Dad, he soon adjusted to his new surroundings and was able to sleep through till morning. But on that one night, if only the aide hadn't shown up, he and John might have made it over the wall!

SECTION IV
Dad's Goodbye

CHAPTER 32
Dad's Legacy

2 Timothy 4:7 *I have fought a good fight, I have finished my course, I have kept the faith.*

Dad was a simple man. I don't mean that he wasn't smart. Quite the opposite. He was valedictorian of his high school graduating class, and he was great at helping me with my homework. He could figure out how to fix or build anything. When he worked for the post office, he could quote the manual verbatim, and he knew where every Texas town was located, no matter how small. However, his needs and wants were simple, and he sometimes didn't understand the complexities of the modern world. He didn't leave behind a collection of awards and trophies or a big estate, but he left behind a legacy of peace and love that will live for a long time.

Dad was hard to buy for because he didn't need much to be happy. If he had a pair of shoes for work and another for Sunday, he didn't see the need of another pair for his birthday. He didn't understand why Givenchy for Men was better than Aqua Velva or Old Spice, and the stylish shirts and sweaters he received for Christmas or Father's Day hung in the back of his closet while he wore his favorite button-up plaid shirts. He played golf with a set of used clubs, and he docked his used fishing boat in a boathouse he'd built with his own hands.

Christmas of 1957 was a memorable one. When he opened his present from Jim and me, he was more excited about that gift than any I had ever seen him open. We had a brand-new Plymouth, maybe the first new car Dad had ever owned. In those days, outside mirrors were an accessory, and one on each side was a real luxury. That year,

Jim and I pooled our money and bought Dad a matching pair of chrome mirrors. He opened the present with a half-smile that said, *Oh, goody, another pair of shoes,* but when he saw the glitter of chrome, he broke into a real smile. When he saw the second mirror, he absolutely beamed.

The working world was almost as confusing to him as the world of fashion. Oh, he understood the work inside out. He knew what he was expected to do, and he did it flawlessly, on time, and without complaint. What he didn't understand was the political gamesmanship and the good ole boys' network that often meant the difference between getting the promotion and getting passed over. He progressed steadily in his career, but the big managerial positions eluded him for years. Finally, as he neared retirement, he was appointed postmaster of a small post office in Trinidad, Texas. It was not a prestigious appointment, but it was a nice little town near his home on Cedar Creek Lake, and there was no doubt he was happy. The local newspaper printed a story of his appointment, and the accompanying picture showed that, once again, he was beaming.

Daddy passed away on May 13, 2011 at the age of 89, less than five months after he moved into Southridge Village. His physical legacy didn't amount to much. He left a 1997 Buick Skylark with low mileage and a pretty good set of tires. He left an old .22 caliber rifle and a beat-up, old shotgun, and he left a small box of old toys, report cards, letters, and assorted memories. He left several boxes of tools and an odd assortment of nails, screws, and other hardware he had collected, just in case. He left a couple of inexpensive watches and a wardrobe that fit in two boxes and two large trash bags when it was taken to Goodwill. He left a retirement annuity and a small savings account that would take care of Mom, but there would be nothing left to pass on to his heirs when she was gone. Finally, he left a plain, gold wedding band.

When Mom and Dad married in 1940, they didn't have enough money for fancy jewelry. He didn't have a ring, and Mom's rings were so thin they wore completely through after twenty years or so. On their twenty-fifth anniversary, Dad presented his bride with a white gold band set with two rows of diamonds, and she presented him with a plain yellow gold band. I never saw him take it off. That band represented the defining reality of his life—his love for Mom. He loved her as Paul told the Ephesians to love their wives, and he would have given up his life for her. He told her every day how beautiful she was and how much he loved her, and he never tired of kissing her or holding her hand.

On May 7, Southridge Village, where he and Mom lived, gave a tea in honor of Mother's Day. Families were invited to come, and Jim and his wife, Jo Lynn, were there. Mom and Dad enjoyed the food and the company, but they didn't have much to say.

"Dad," Jim said when they finished eating, "did you do anything exciting today?"

Dad thought a minute and then smiled. "I kissed your mother."

That was the last intelligible thing either of us heard him say. He suffered a major stroke later that night.

His last few days were spent under hospice care in the room he shared with Mom. Their double bed was moved out to make room for a hospital bed for him and a twin bed for her. Her bed went unused as she climbed into bed with him each night. He slept most of the time, but when he occasionally woke up, he indicated with nods or shakes of his head that he was comfortable and was not in any pain. The day before he died, he spent most of the day on his side with his face toward the wall. I encouraged Mom to move up beside his bed so he could see her. He opened his eyes, and his face lit up with the love that always shone in his eyes when he looked at her.

"Hi," she said, patting his face and smiling back at him.

"Hi," he mouthed back, even though no sound came out.

The love that began in the cotton fields of West Texas over seven decades before was still strong. It was stronger than the years, stronger than the physical infirmities, stronger than the dementia.

The next morning, we were getting ready for our daily visit when we got a call. "You need to come right now." Daddy had passed away quietly that morning. With an aide holding his hand, he had simply stopped breathing.

No matter how expected it is, the final goodbye is always hard. We cried as we sat on the twin bed looking at the empty shell that had been our dad.

"Grandmother Robinson has her whole family with her in Heaven now," I said.

Dad was the next to the youngest in a family of nine children, and he was the last to go home. He was a man of strong faith who believed in Jesus as his Savior, and he died with the peace of knowing where he was going.

Dad didn't look all that different after he died. Most of the life had already drained out of him, but the little bit that was left went peacefully with no signs of struggle. His mouth was open as if he were snoring, but there was no movement, no blinking, no breathing. This was my first experience with death up close, but Jim is a minister.

"I've attended many deathbeds, but this one is as peaceful as I've ever seen," he said.

Later, we met with the social worker who would be overseeing Mom's financial and living situation. After what we thought was a routine meeting, she closed her file, folded her hands on top of it, and took a deep breath.

"I want to thank you. I've been through a lot of situations like this, but rarely do I see this much peace. All of you are obviously at peace with each other, at peace with the situation, and at peace with your God. That makes my job so much easier."

Along with his legacy of love, Dad had left us with a legacy of peace. We had learned to love each other and to live at peace with each other and with our circumstances. We were able to release him with no regrets, knowing nothing was left unsaid or undone. We said goodbye for now, knowing that when our time comes, he will be there waiting to show us the way.

CHAPTER 33
Death Is Not a Simple Business

Genesis 23:19 *And after this, Abraham buried Sarah his wife in the cave of the field of Machpelah before Mamre.*

Dad's death was fairly simple. He had a massive stroke, and a few days later, he stopped breathing. The business of death, however, is another story. Months and even years later, my brother and I were still dealing with paperwork.

There was a time when a loved one died, he was laid out on the dining room table for the wake and buried under an oak tree in the back forty. There were no officials, bureaucrats, or businessmen demanding attention and decisions at a time when those left behind are least prepared to deal with them. There was time to grieve and quietly reflect on the life that had slipped out of reach. Times have changed.

When Dad died, before my face had completely dried from the first torrent of tears, hospice came to pronounce him dead, the coroner came to fill out the proper forms, a social worker came to discuss Mom's situation as his survivor, and a gentleman from the local funeral home came to begin the process of laying Dad to rest. Forgive my cynicism, but I'm pretty sure the smile on his face slipped a bit when we told him Dad would be buried in Dallas. He quickly recovered his poise though, presented us with the appropriate forms for signature, and quietly proceeded with his duties.

The next item on the agenda was selecting a burial outfit. I went through Dad's closet, choosing a suit, shirt, and tie. I had done the same thing for him many Sunday mornings in the six years he and Mom had lived with us, but this time, I was extra careful in my choices. This was the last time I would do it. With the selections made and approved by my brother, we made sure Mom was settled in before we went to the funeral home. We gave the receptionist our names and sat quietly in the reception area, lost in our own thoughts. In a few minutes, the funeral director came out to greet us.

"Are you here for Mr. Robinson?"

"Yes."

"He's already on his way to Texas." Modern efficiency doesn't leave much time for meditation.

"But I have his suit," I said.

"Don't worry. We dressed him in suitable traveling attire."

I didn't ask what that meant. I didn't want to think about my modest dad, somewhere between Conway and Dallas, like a Norman Mailer novel, naked and dead.

A few days later, we met with the funeral director in Dallas. The pre-need policy Dad had purchased many years before specified the basics, but there were still decisions to be made: flowers, marker, choice of chapel, time of visitation and service, programs for the service, thank you notes, and honorariums. We kept it as simple as possible, but there was still more paperwork than a house closing.

The day of the service, the paperwork was forgotten as we said goodbye to Dad with dignity and love. He was dressed in his best suit.

Then, it got complicated. There's an electronic network that quickly notifies the world at large of a death. Dad's Social Security and pension deposits immediately stopped, and when I tried to transfer money into Mom's credit union, it was blocked and the account was marked as a "death account." That's where the quick part of the electronic network ended. Some of my exchanges with the credit union follow, in chronological, if not logical, order.

"I can make that transfer for you. Then we can change the account to your mom's name and keep the same account number."

She was so helpful, and under the circumstances, I really appreciated her kindness.

"I'm waiting for a death certificate so I can close the account."

I didn't want to close the account. She must have misplaced her notes about our last conversation. I knew she had a lot to do.

"Your mom is joint owner on the account, but she's not a credit union member. You'll have to fill out an application."

Why didn't she tell me that the first time we talked? I still couldn't transfer money into Mom's account, and we were back at square one.

"We have your power of attorney for your dad on file but not for your mom. You'll have to send those again and let our legal department review them."

Oh great! Now the attorneys were involved.

"We had to open the account under a new number. It shouldn't be a problem."

The retirement home might have disagreed with her. I'd let the credit union explain why their automatic draft bounced.

"Your brother needs to sign the application, too."

JUST. SEND. THE. STUPID. FORMS—again.

Finally, my part of the paperwork was done, but Jim was not so fortunate. As executor of Dad's will, he had the responsibility of dealing with Social Security, Medicaid, and Dad's USPS pension fund. He straightened out the Social Security survivor benefits after opening *another* account in Arkansas, Mom's current state of residence, but Medicaid required several trips on the governmental merry-go-round. The application Jim had submitted before Dad died had to be redone, omitting Dad's information and including Mom's new income figures. He completed and submitted the new application, and even received confirmation, but when he followed up, the only paperwork that could be found was the joint application. It was enough to drive my easygoing brother, who rarely raises his voice, even in the pulpit, into a near-raging come-apart and into enlisting the services of an attorney.

The most difficult problems, however, involved the monthly survivor benefits Mom was supposed to get from Dad's retirement. Many rounds of erroneous and lost paperwork left all concerned waiting for retroactive benefits to be paid. Mom's savings ran out long before the issues were resolved, and her reduced income wasn't enough to cover her bills. Fortunately, due in part to their desire to provide the best care for their residents and in part to their contributions to some of the errors, Southridge Village was willing to wait for payment.

One evening, while we were all still trapped in red tape, David and I watched the movie "Spencer's Mountain." Grandpa died, and after the funeral, Grandma called the family together. She flipped open a writing tablet and read the will Grandpa had dictated to her the night before he died. There was no probate, no contest, and no rules and regulations. There's a lot to be said about the simplicity with which the business of death was carried out in the good old days.

CHAPTER 34
What's in a Tombstone

Genesis 35:19–20 [19]*And Rachel died…*[20]*And Jacob set a pillar upon her grave.*

Several months after Dad died, David and I drove the sixty miles from Emory to Dallas to the cemetery where Dad was buried. I wanted to be sure his marker had been installed and everything was printed correctly.

During the drive, I had lots of time to think about grave markers and what they mean. I had watched a movie the week before involving several graves that were marked with piles of stones and two sticks tied together in the shape of a cross—quite a difference from the private mausoleum that sits just inside the entrance to the section of Restland where Dad is buried. It's about the size of a large walk-in closet, is made of polished marble, and has at least one stained glass window. It's set on a small plot of ground separated from the rest of the cemetery by a wrought iron fence. It would appear that good fences make good neighbors even in death.

Dad's marker is less elaborate—a lot less elaborate. Like all the markers in his area, his is flat against the ground so the lawn mowers can go right across it. It's an attractive brass plate, about 18" X 24", give or take a few inches. It's adorned with dogwood blossoms and has his name, date of birth, and date of death. Below that are the words "Together Forever" followed by Mom's name and dates. They had a "duplex" plot, so she could be buried on top of him when her time came. It's what they had chosen when they purchased their preneed plan forty years before.

As I thought about rough wooden crosses, elaborate marble monuments, and simple brass plaques, I wondered why we feel a need to mark the place where our last remains will slowly return to the dust from which they came. I guess it's a way of saying *I was here. Remember me.* I'm not sure I want to remember Dad that way though. Standing in the Garden of Reflections with the fountain bubbling behind me, I remembered him in his casket. He looked as natural as the mortician's arts could make him. They had even caught the hint of a mischievous smile on his face, like he was about to tell a corny joke—but his hair was too puffy on top, he had on makeup, and the wire support holding his head in place was visible. I'd much rather remember him by looking at photo albums, telling stories about him at family gatherings, or seeing him in the faces of his grandsons.

There's one other feature on his marker—a built-in vase. The vase is hidden below the surface, but we can pull in out, turn it over, and screw it into place if we want to put flowers in it. There's a whole industry that has grown up around filling these little vases. Around Memorial Day and other national holidays, end caps spring up in many stores offering memorial bouquets of artificial flowers in patriotic colors, and cemeteries across the country are festooned with these bouquets, flags, balloons, and other objects of tribute. It has become our way of honoring and paying our respects to our departed loved ones.

At the risk of sounding like the cemetery cynic, who are we doing it for? The loved one is certainly not there to enjoy our tributes, and once the holiday is over, the groundskeepers are the only ones who see them. I honored and respected my dad when he was alive, and I continue to do so by living the type of moral and ethical life he taught me to live.

I don't visit Dad's grave or take flowers. Restland is close to the intersection of LBJ Freeway and Central Expressway, one of the busiest snarls of concrete and steel in the Dallas area, so driving there is not much fun. His little area is attractive enough, but there are no benches or shade trees to make it an inviting place to linger and meditate. Since Restland is a perpetual care cemetery, there won't be a need for family "cemetery workings" to weed, trim, and otherwise beautify his site. Wherever I am, though, whether it's at home, on the road in the RV, or looking at his little brass marker, I'll carry his memory in my heart and honor the man I called Daddy.

SECTION V
Mom's Last Year

CHAPTER 35
False Alarms

Psalm 112:7 *He shall not be afraid of evil tidings: his heart is fixed, trusting in the LORD.*

My cell phone doesn't ring much. I've never been a real chatty person, especially on the phone, and I'm getting worse as I get older. As much as I hate to admit it, I don't hear as well on the phone as I used to. I'd like to blame it on my old phone or the poor connection we sometimes get among the many trees where we live, but whatever the reason, I end up saying, "Huh?" and "What was that?" a lot more often than I'd like. When my phone rings, I'm usually in Wal-Mart, and David is calling from the automotive or electronics department wondering when I'll be ready to check out. That's why, when my phone rang one afternoon a couple of months after Dad died and the caller ID showed a number with the area code where Mom lived, a jolt of apprehension twisted my stomach into a knot.

"Hello."

"Mrs. Brendle?"

"Yes."

"This is Southridge Village where you mother lives. I wanted to let you know that Mrs. Robinson has been throwing up blood, and we called an ambulance to take her to the emergency room to get her checked out."

"Have you called my brother?" He lived about three miles from Southridge.

"We weren't able to contact him, but we spoke to his wife. She's going to meet the ambulance at the hospital. We'll call you as soon as we know anything."

"Okay. Thanks."

One of the hardest parts of being a long-distance caregiver is the waiting. While you wait, you worry. Is it serious? Is she in pain? Is she scared? Should we jump in the car and head that way? Another hard part is the imagination running wild. Maybe it's a bleeding ulcer. That's pretty easy to fix, isn't it? On the other hand, she's been putting on a lot of weight lately. Maybe she has a tumor in her abdomen. Maybe it's the Big C. Maybe it's...

My phone rang again. It was my sister-in-law.

"Hello."

"Hi. It's Jo Lynn. Did Southridge get in touch with you?"

"Yes, they called a little while ago. Any news yet?"

"No, I just got to the hospital, and the ambulance just arrived."

"Did you get hold of Jim?"

"Yes. He's on the lake, fishing with Sean. I'll call him back as soon as I find out what's going on."

The tension in her voice was audible. She had lost both her parents two years before, and we had just lost Dad. Now, here she was again, at the hospital.

"I'm sorry you're having to go through this alone."

"It's okay. I just hope they'll let me sign the papers for her. I'll call you."

The next phone call was from Jim.

"Hello."

"Hey, I think we're okay. I talked with the staff at Southridge, and they had spaghetti for dinner. The staff nurse had left for the day. I'm hoping they were just being overly cautious. I'll let you know."

He called back a few minutes later.

"The doctor came in while I was on the phone with you. She wasn't throwing up blood. It was marinara sauce."

It was going to be funny once the adrenaline settled down.

"We've made some other discoveries, too," Jim continued. "I talked with the nurse about Mom's weight, and she agreed to cut down on her portions a little bit. But they've also been watching her table a little more closely."

The residents were seated at tables for four in the dining room, and Mom shared her meals with her three best friends. One of them was a mother-hen type who believed in clean plates.

"It seems that Mom cleans not only her plate," said Jim, "but also, at the encouragement of her friend, everyone else's plate at the table. She also spends a lot of time in her friend's apartment, and that place looks like a candy store. You know how little impulse control Mom has. It's no wonder she's gained weight."

So, marinara sauce instead of blood. Leftovers and candy instead of a growing tumor. Good news. Relief. Until the next phone call.

CHAPTER 36
Where Did She Go?

John 7:34 *Ye shall seek me, and shall not find me.*

All of us, especially those of us who are in the second half-century of life, have had the experience of misplacing our keys or wallet temporarily. We think, *Now where did that go,* and sometimes we worry. We think it might be the sign of something sinister, but according to the experts, it's a normal part of aging. A person with Alzheimer's Disease is likely to be more creative in misplacing things, like putting an iron in the freezer or a wristwatch in the sugar bowl. The first time I was aware of Mom's creative storage practices was when I asked to use her hair spray.

"Sure," she said. "It's under the mattress."

Following her directions, I found it in her bedroom, nestled between the mattress and box springs.

"Why do you keep it there?"

"To keep it cool."

Well, of course. Silly me!

I began to find other things in strange places. There were empty makeup jars and bottles tucked between the mattresses along with the hair spray, and her usually organized kitchen was a study in creative disorder. I visited her at lunch every day, and when I went to her kitchen to get a glass or a bowl, it was like a game of hide and seek.

The game continued in my kitchen when Mom and Dad moved in with us. They wanted to pull their weight, so they set the table before meals and did the dishes afterward—and I began the preparation for every meal with a search for the particular pot or pan

I wanted. Cereal was likely to be found under the island with the small appliances instead of in the pantry, and ice cream sometimes ended up in the vegetable crisper. I learned to do a kitchen sweep as soon as The Kids finished their chores.

The same confusion reigned in her closet and drawers. A session of organizing that took me several hours could be undone by one quick session of rooting as Mom searched for an item she had already forgotten. Then, when she tried to replace the things she had dragged out, there was no method to her madness. Socks ended up in the night stand, underwear was stashed in the desk, pantyhose were put in her purse—and the purse was an issue all by itself.

Paranoia is not listed on the Alzheimer's websites as one of the normal symptoms, but Mom was paranoid, especially about her purse. She sometimes left it on her night stand or on the sofa, but more often, she hid it. I usually didn't have a problem finding it because I knew all her hiding places: on a hanger in the back of the closet, under her underwear in the chest of drawers, or her old favorite, between the mattress and box springs.

One time, though, she outdid herself. The purse disappeared, and I couldn't find it. I looked in all the usual places, and it wasn't there. She had an appointment coming up with a new doctor, and all her ID and insurance cards were in her wallet, so it was critical I find it. I made a search that would have looked good on NCIS, and still no luck. Finally, when I was stripping the sheets off their bed, a little purse strap popped out between the mattress and headboard. She had put it under the mattress, wedged up far enough that I missed it. Maybe I'm not NCIS material after all.

There's something else I wasn't able to find. Earlier, I recounted an incident when Mom and I were singing. As we sang an old, familiar hymn, our eyes met, and just for a moment, she was there. Then, she slipped away again, and I didn't see much of her after that.

The movie "Temple Grandin" is about an amazing woman who became very successful in spite of autism, but she struggled with some of the intangibles in life. When faced with the death of a favorite horse, of the cattle in a slaughter house where she was doing research, and of a beloved teacher, she stared at the lifeless bodies and asked the question that troubles a lot of us. *Where did they go?*

Mom had beautiful brown eyes that were once deep and expressive, revealing her love, joy, disappointments, and fears. As Alzheimer's made more inroads into her brain, her eyes were usually blank and empty. They lit up when someone came in and gave her a hug or told her it was time to go to the dining room. They even showed glimmers of recognition occasionally, but the glimmers were short lived, and as they faded, I was left wondering, *where did she go*?

CHAPTER 37
A Dream and a Birthday Party

Psalm 56:3 *What time I am afraid, I will trust in Thee.*

The week after Mom's ninetieth birthday, I dreamed about her and Dad. I often dreamed about them as my subconscious worked through the grief of Dad's death and the nagging guilt that caregivers feel about how this decision could have been resolved differently or that situation could have been handled better. When I woke up at 4:30, the dream was clear, but after a few hours and a little more sleep, the details faded into the foggy confusion that makes up foreign art films. The only thing that remained clear was that Mom and Dad were, once again, coming to live with me. It wasn't on my list of Top Ten Favorite Dreams.

The dream probably came from my visit to Mom the previous weekend. She had celebrated her birthday on Saturday, and a small group of family and friends gathered to celebrate with her. I had been skeptical about the idea at first, envisioning a lot of work and no small amount of chaos. Once again, I worried too much. Jo Lynn used her Creative Memory talents to create a nostalgic invitation, and Southridge Village took care of the party details. Two of Mom's remaining three sisters came, along with a niece, her husband, and a nephew. A local grandson came with his two children, and two couples from Jim's church showed up. It was a small but lively group, large enough to show the respect merited by ninety years but not so large as to overwhelm Mom's already confused mind.

Jo Lynn and I bought Mom a new pantsuit and a corsage of red roses for the occasion. After she visited the on-site salon for a shampoo and style, I applied a touch of blusher, eye shadow, and lipstick for a little additional glamour. I had always enjoyed our girl times when she was with me, and she never lost her love of being pampered.

Once preparations were finished, she was ready to party. She made her grand entrance with a huge smile that never left her face. She had no idea what was going on, but she knew she was the center of a lot of attention, and she loved every minute of it. In spite of a "No Gifts" note on the invitation, there were a few packages to open. Her favorite was a stuffed cat from her great-granddaughter Emma Leigh. In quiet moments, she held it in her lap and absently stroked its soft fur.

There were lots of cameras, and picture time was hilarious. Aunt Grace also had Alzheimer's, and while Mom's personality had subsided into smiling compliance, Aunt Grace was still a live wire. She talked constantly, sometimes apparently speaking in tongues. She gestured emphatically with her hands, and she was rarely still for more than a few seconds at a time. Posing the sisters was like trying to hold three corks underwater at the same time. We started out with the birthday girl in the middle, but that didn't work out very well. Aunt Fay, the youngest and the only sound mind in the group, moved to the middle and tried to corral the other two. The resulting photos were endearing, if not portrait quality.

The party was a rousing success, and I was glad Jim and Jo Lynn's optimism had won out over my doubt. There was another aspect to the weekend, though—the caregiver part. Friday night, Jim and Jo Lynn hosted a dinner at their home for those of us who had come to town early. While they got everything ready, David and I went to get Mom. I easily fell back into my familiar role. I walked her to the car, offering my arm for support, eased her into the front seat of our two-door Grand Prix, and fastened her seat belt. During the evening, I enjoyed sitting by her, holding her hand, and interacting with her in her limited way—but I also took her to the bathroom, helped her with her dinner, and put her to bed when we took her back to Southridge. By the time we got back to our motel, I was exhausted. I was also feeling some guilty twinges about the relief I felt at turning her back over to her professional caregivers.

Maybe that was where the dream came from. There was a fear that, at some point, the financial resources might run out, or for some other reason, Mom might no longer be able to stay at Southridge. Considering how I felt after the weekend, I wasn't sure I was physically or emotionally up to the task of caring for her. There was also the guilty realization that I didn't really want to resume my role as her primary caregiver. As much as I cherished the years I was able to care for her and Dad, that time had passed, and I now cherished the time David and I had together.

Back in my own home, in the bright sunshine of a Texas morning, as the night visions faded, I thought about the many Bible verses that say, "Do not fear." I remembered the caregiver support group discussions about false guilt, and I tried to put it behind me. It was, after all, only a dream.

CHAPTER 38
I'm Addicted to Caregiving

1 Peter 5:7 *Casting all your care upon Him; for He careth for you.*

A few months after Mom's birthday, David and I spent several days around New Year's with Jim. We enjoy spending time with him and Jo Lynn. They're a fun couple who always has neat ideas of interesting things to do, and they are excellent hosts. That alone would have been enough of an incentive for a visit, but they also lived three miles from Southridge. I missed Mom a lot, but in the twelve months since she and Dad had left our home, I had begun to recover both my sanity and my health and to remember how much I enjoyed spending uninterrupted time with David. However, our New Year's visit confirmed that it was a good thing she lived almost three hundred miles away because I was just a step away from relapsing into addiction. Hi, my name is Linda, and I'm a caregiver.

We arrived at Jim's around dinnertime on Wednesday, too late to visit Mom. Southridge served dinner early, and she usually went to bed shortly after she ate. In addition, she suffered from Sundowners Syndrome along with her Alzheimer's, so as the sun set, so did what little coherency she had left. Thursday morning, my addiction kicked in, and I was ready to go see her as soon as we finished breakfast. When I walked into the day room on Mom's wing, I saw one of the residents at a table, asleep over her unfinished breakfast, and Mom with her hand in the lady's plate. A staff member was trying to gently coax Mom away from the table and over to the sofa to watch "The Price Is Right." This was my chance to slip back into my role, and the staff member, recognizing the gleam in my eye, gladly relinquished her charge.

"Hi, Mom. It's Linda."

She looked at me in confusion for a moment, and a flood of emotion filled her eyes. It would be stretching it to say she recognized me, but there was enough familiarity to trigger a response, and that was enough for me. We hugged for a long time, and I led her to her apartment where we could sit and visit.

"Where are your glasses, Mom?"

It was obvious from the blank look on her face, that she had no idea what glasses I was talking about much less where they were. Later, when I asked an aide about them, she said they had been missing for a couple of months. I imagine keeping glasses on a ninety-year-old woman with Alzheimer's is like trying to keep shoes on a toddler, so I put it out of my mind and focused on enjoying my visit.

As I held Mom's hand, I realized how sticky it was and how dirty her nails were. Grazing off other people's plates is dirty work. If any of my caregiver persona was still in hiding, it sprang forth in full strength. I found some wet wipes in the bathroom and went to work, but one small taste always leads to another. I noticed that her nails were a little ragged, so I found a nail clipper and evened them up a bit. Then, I mainlined, pulling off her shoes and checking her toenails. Before I knew it, I was sitting on the floor at her feet surrounded by clippings. All too soon, it was lunch time, so I hugged her goodbye with promises of another visit tomorrow.

Friday was the day of the big New Year's dinner, so we delayed our visit until five o'clock. I didn't have to wait long for my caregiving fix once we got there. Mom was already seated at our table, and the table was preset with salads and desserts. She was always an eat-dessert-first kind of girl, and she was wrist deep in a chocolate cupcake covered with fluffy, white frosting and chocolate sauce. I wiped her hands and face the best I could with a napkin but left it to a staff member to clean her up with a wet wipe. There were plenty of caregiving opportunities left for me, though: salad to be dressed, prime rib to be cut up, baked potato to be prepared, wine glass to be filled with sparkling apple juice. By the time we finished eating and moved to the fireplace to take family photos, I was flying high. When Jo Lynn and I walked Mom to her room, I didn't even feel the need to dress her for bed. I was satisfied with sitting her down in front of the TV, covering her with a light blanket, and leaving the nighttime duties to the paid personnel—a victory of sorts for an addict like me.

Saturday was another story. David and I went for a visit around midmorning, planning to spend an hour or two before lunch. I expected to find Mom with her friends in the day room, watching TV or having a snack, but instead, I found her in bed. She was napping in a T-shirt and her underwear, so I woke her gently and went into my best caregiver mode. I took her to the bathroom and started to help her get dressed. When I took off her shirt, I was horrified by the red welts and scabs where she had scratched raw spots on her stomach, shoulders, and back. I had battled similar problems when she was with me, going through countless tubes of cortisone and antibiotic cream and reminding her endlessly not to scratch, but it was never this bad. I felt the familiar pangs of guilt and doubt, wondering once again if I should have kept her with me and if she was being neglected.

Sunday was a repeat of Saturday, except it was afternoon and Mom was napping fully dressed. Monday morning, we left for home, and we stopped by Southridge for one more visit. I went by the nurse's office before going to Mom's apartment and asked about the things that concerned me.

"Are we supposed to clip her toenails, or is that something you do here?"

"If you'll tell the CNA on her wing and be sure there are clippers in her room, we'll take care of it."

"Do you have a lost and found where we might find her glasses?"

"Not specifically, but I'll put a note in the communication log to check again and see if we can find them."

"Are you aware of the terrible rash she has on her chest, stomach, and back?"

"Yes," she said as she pulled Mom's file. "The doctor put her on an antibiotic about six weeks ago, but that didn't help. He thinks it's more nerve related, so he put her on Risperdal in December. I'll be sure he looks at it again on his next visit, and I'll note all your concerns in the communication log to be sure everyone is aware of the situation."

Satisfied I had done all I could, I spent an hour or so with Mom, brushing graham cracker crumbs off the front of her shirt and guessing prices along with Drew Carey. When it was time to leave, I gave her one last hug.

"We have to go now, Mom. They'll be coming to get you for lunch in a few minutes. I love you."

"Okay. I love you, too."

She smiled contentedly and turned her attention back to the TV. As we headed toward Texas, I felt the pangs of withdrawal, worrying about her toenails, her glasses, her rash, not knowing if or when I would see her again in this life. I, once again, pried my fingers off the controls, knowing that Jim and the Southridge staff were perfectly capable of caring for her. I thought about the Serenity Prayer that is often used in twelve-step programs to help those in recovery let go of their addictions.

I focused on the blessings of my visit, the momentary recognition in her eyes, the constant smile of contentment that lit her face, the moment when she cupped my face in both her hands and said, "You're beautiful." I let all the sorrows fall away, and by the time we got home, the anxiety had lessened and my addiction was once again under control. I eventually learned to let go of the caregiving without letting go of the caring. It was slow going, but I just took it one day at a time.

CHAPTER 39
The Phone Calls I Hate

2 Corinthians 5:8 *We are confident, I say, and willing rather to be absent from the body, and to be present with the Lord.*

Phone calls can have many meanings to a caregiver or anyone whose loved one is aging or in ill health. I wrote earlier about a phone call that turned out to be a false alarm. Instead of blood, Mom was throwing up marinara sauce. In March, after our New Year's party, I received a couple of calls that weren't *the* phone call, but they weren't false alarms either. After the calls ended, words like *we may be out of options* and *this is sometimes the beginning of the final episode* continued to haunt me.

The skin eruptions I had noticed in December had continued to plague Mom. The initial diagnosis had been shingles, but it was changed to Bullous Pemphigoid (BP). BP is an autoimmune disease similar to Lupus, except it affects only the skin instead of internal organs. The biggest problem was the itch, and like a child, Mom couldn't keep from scratching. As a result, she had been in and out of the hospital, fighting the infection the scratching caused. To complicate matters, her chronic urinary tract infection (UTI) had shown up again, and the treatments for the BP and the UTI were not always compatible. At ninety years old, her body could only tolerate so much, and the doctor had said a couple of times that "if this doesn't work, we may be out of options." Thankfully, as of March, it was working. The UTI seemed to be under control, and no new blisters had appeared in a couple of days.

Another problem had arisen, though. As Alzheimer's progresses, it sometimes affects the ability to swallow. After noticing that Mom was wheezing a bit, the doctor ran more tests and discovered she was aspirating her food. That's a fancy way of saying her food was going down the wrong pipe. The aspiration had caused a small spot of pneumonia, so she was facing another course of treatment that might or might not work and that she might or might not be able to tolerate. Jim said that she was alert, happy, and even more aware of who he was than normal, but no one could predict how long that would last. Jim called and e-mailed daily, and more often when there was news. Still, I needed to see her in person, to love on her, to hold her hand. So, David and I planned another trip to Arkansas.

I hated what that implied—that if I didn't go immediately, she might not recognize me the next time. Even worse, her condition might suddenly deteriorate, and I might not get a chance to say goodbye. However, one lesson I had learned as a caregiver was that denial didn't work. You had to face the fact that no matter how good a job you did, how much you prayed, how many positive thoughts you had, your loved one would eventually die.

I'm not afraid of death, but I fear the process. As a conservative and sometimes fundamental Christian, I believe what Jesus said about death and the life to come.

John 14: 2–3 *In my Father's house are many mansions: if it were not so, I would have told you. I go to prepare a place for you. And if I go and prepare a place for you, I will come again, and receive you unto myself; that where I am, there ye may be also.*

In addition to the Bible, books have been written and movies have been made about encounters with the hereafter, near-death experiences, a white light, departed loved ones, feelings of love and acceptance. The best stories, however, are the ones friends tell about the death of their loved ones. These are the ones that really reinforce the belief that the best is yet to come.

My favorite is about a friend who had a long hard battle with cancer. As the end neared, he lapsed into a coma. Then, one night, he smiled without opening his eyes.

"It's so beautiful. There are flowers everywhere," he said. His smile widened even further, and he started waving as if in greeting. Then, he died.

Another friend tells of her mother's death. Just before she died, as she lay there with her family surrounding her, she smiled and said, "Yes, Lord. I hear you."

I believed that when Mom's time came, she would truly be home, in a better place where she would be well and happy. Still, I dreaded the process that would take her there. I hated that she had spent three of the last six weeks in the hospital. I hated that she had to eat pureed food and drink thickened water and that she had to endure endless needle sticks, even when her old, delicate veins collapsed. As caregivers do, though, I planned to do what I could. I would visit; I would consult with Jim and the doctors; I would pray, and I would leave Mom in the hands of the One who loved her more than I ever could.

CHAPTER 40
Ready or Not

Matthew 24:44 *Therefore be ye also ready: for in such an hour as ye think not the Son of man cometh.*

Hide and Seek is a favorite game of children. One child is designated as "It," and while the other children run and hide, "It" stays at "base," hides his eyes, and counts. When he reaches thirty or fifty or one hundred, he yells, "Ready or not, here I come." Those few words evoke lots of emotions in the other children. If they've not yet found a suitable hiding place, they feel panic as they realize they're completely exposed and in danger of being caught. If they have hidden daringly close to base, they feel a thrill of fear and excitement as they anticipate that mad dash to safety, trying to avoid being tagged. Those who have found the *perfect* hiding place may be overcome with giggles as they realize that "It" has no chance of finding them. I don't play Hide and Seek much anymore except with my grandchildren, but through the years, I've encountered many situations that have yelled, "Ready or not, here I come," especially situations arising from caring for loved ones.

That's how I felt on our visit to Arkansas. Mom had been in the hospital for two weeks this time, and the charge nurse said she would be there at least two more. It had been a rough few weeks, and we met with hospice.

Nobody had given us a timeline or pointed out an expiration date on the bottom of her foot, but she had been moved to the long-term care wing of the hospital. Jim and I, along with our super-supportive spouses, had been looking at options for when she was released. We visited with the staff at the assisted living facility where Mom lived to discuss care options if she returned there, and we visited a skilled nursing facility to see what services they offered in case she needed more intensive care. Still, at least in my mind, we had been talking about how to get her back to the place she was before she went into the hospital, how to get her back to feeding herself regular food instead of being fed purees and nectar thickened drinks, how to get her walking again instead of sitting in a chair a couple of hours a day with help. The hospice nurse we met with put a great big pin in that bubble.

I thought I was being realistic and that I was ready to face the inevitable—but that was before the hospice nurse started talking about end stage dementia, inpatient hospice, and other emotionally charged subjects. I maintained control, but tears rolled down my face as we continued to discuss options and ask questions. The nurse took contact and other pertinent information and said he would have a note added to Mom's chart. When she was ready to be discharged, the hospital would call hospice to come in and do an evaluation to see if she qualified for their services and to plan how to proceed. It was hard to think about before, but it was harder when he put Mom's name on the form.

We visited with Mom a few more minutes, and as I sat on her bed, holding her hands, she looked at me expectantly.

"Are we ready?" she said.

She raised her head up off the pillow a little bit as if she were trying to get out of bed, and she looked toward the door. Since losing some of her social anxieties to Alzheimer's, she has been ready to go at a moment's notice.

"No," I said. "We're not ready yet."

I said it gently, but inside I was screaming. *No, I'm not ready. I'm not ready for that nurse to say it's possible that no amount of physical therapy will get you back on your feet again. I'm not ready to hear that you may have to eat pureed food from now on. I'm not ready.*

Later, after we left the hospital and returned to Jim's for the night, I spent some time examining my feelings. I thought about the changes

I had seen in Mom in the last year and how the things the nurse talked about were the next steps in a natural progression. I thought about sitting on Mom's bed the day before as she drifted in and out of sleep. At the time, I thought, *if she closed her eyes right now and simply stopped breathing, I could handle that.* I thought of all the love and support we had, and I thought about all the systems that were in place to help us through the process. I realized I was feeling the panic of the child who hasn't found a hiding place and feels exposed when the call comes. As I meditated, I became calmer. I came to the realization that, like it or not, when "It" called out "Ready or not, here I come," I would be ready. I had no choice.

CHAPTER 41
The Healing Power of Spring, Harleys, and Riding Mowers

Psalm 30:5 *Weeping may endure for a night, but joy cometh in the morning.*

I went into emotional hibernation after we returned home from Arkansas. People who have loved ones in the end stages of any disease are grieving a loss that's not over yet, so there is no closure. Sometimes, it's hard to think or talk or write about anything else, and sometimes, it becomes a real downer for you and everyone around you, regardless of how loving, understanding, and supportive they are. So, you try not to write or talk, or even think. Still, the human spirit is resilient and continues to seek healing wherever it's available. I found a bit of healing a week later as David and I took a ride on the Harley and went shopping for a riding lawn mower.

I'm a firm believer in the therapeutic effects of riding a motorcycle. Riding along at sixty or seventy miles an hour will blow the worries right out of your head, and it will make you more aware of God's beautiful creation as well. I rode my own bike for several years, but since coming in second in an inadvertent game of chicken with a dump truck, I've been riding on the back behind David. I miss the feeling of control and independence riding solo gave me, but I enjoy the closeness of riding two up and the chance it gives me to really enjoy the scenery. Seeing the countryside on the back of a bike instead of through the window of a car is like seeing a movie on IMAX instead of on a small TV screen, only better. There's no limit to the size of the screen, there's real surround sound, and there's even smell-o-vision. The smell of freshly cut grass and wild flowers is God's own aroma therapy. I could do without the skunks and livestock pens, but holding your breath is supposed to increase lung capacity, so even that's not bad.

The day we went for a ride was a perfect day. Texas was actually having spring that year. Sometimes, Texas weather goes directly from cold to hot with no mild days in between, but that year, we had some spring rains and a number of open-window days. It might have been because we had no real winter to speak of. I was hoping the mild winter wasn't a sign that triple-digit temperatures would be arriving early. Whatever the meteorological reasons, it was an ideal day for a ride, and shopping for a mower was all the excuse we needed.

When we lived in Florida, we had a nice civilized yard with St. Augustine grass and defined flower beds. A self-propelled gas mower was all we needed. Then, we moved to a two-plus-acre plot of land in Texas with lots of trees, lots of tree stumps, and lots of weeds. By the middle of the summer, the old mower gave up the ghost, but the drought was in full force, so the weeds died, too. However, with the aforementioned rains, the weeds came back fiercely, and it was time to bring in some heavy artillery. We donned our helmets, climbed on the bike and headed for Sulphur Springs, about twenty miles away. It was a glorious, spirit-lifting ride, but the real healing began when we got to our first stop.

For the first few minutes, I browsed the mowers with David, but cutting widths and engine specs quickly palled, so I wandered into the garden section. I marveled as I always do at the tiny plants that in a few weeks would produce tomatoes, peppers, cucumbers, and all sorts of good things to eat. A mother and her young son were looking at berry vines, and their enthusiasm was contagious.

"I want blueberries," he said.

"I don't think they have blueberries, but they have strawberries," she said.

"Can I have grapes?"

"I don't think grapes are a good idea for us."

"What are figs?"

"It's hard to explain, but you wouldn't like them."

"I want a red one."

They finally settled on two strawberry plants, one raspberry, and one blackberry. I saw cobblers in their future, and I saw the promise of new life.

Before long, David was ready to do a little comparison shopping. At the next store, we were greeted by an enthusiastic salesman. He knew his product, and he knew his customers. He soon had David driving a mower around the parking lot. He looked a little odd wearing his black do rag with orange flames instead of a gimme cap, but I could tell by the look on his face that he had found his ride. While he buzzed around, testing brakes, speed, and all those other guy things, I stood in the shade, enjoying the cool breeze, watching the birds jockey for position on the power lines, and healing a bit more. Then, David made a tight 360 turn as if he was mowing around one of our many trees, and I knew he was sold.

"Do you give veterans' discounts?" he said to the salesman.

"No, but this is last year's model, so we might be able to work something out."

By the time they closed the deal and we mounted up for the ride home, I was really open to what the day had to offer. The fields on either side of the road were thick with green grass and wildflowers instead of the dry brown leftovers of last summer's drought. There were a few trees that still sported bare branches, but most were covered with new leaves or promising buds. The lake was still low, but there was enough water to entice several fishermen to wade out and cast a line. There were fat cows that looked ready to drop a calf at any moment and frisky colts running around the pen. I thought about Mom's life slowly fading away, I thought about the new life springing up all around me, and I thought of what the psalmist said— after the weeping, there is joy.

CHAPTER 42
On Life, Perspective, and Morning Glories

Psalms 121:1 *I will lift up mine eyes unto the hills, from whence cometh my help.*

My friendship with Sue was a sisters-in-arms story. As men become brothers in times of war, Sue and I became sisters on the battlefield of caregiving. We first met at our church in a small group that was studying finances from a Christian perspective. The group bonded well and decided to move on from finances to Rick Warren's study called *The Purpose Driven Church*. During the course of the study, we were challenged to be open to new ministry or service opportunities in which we might become involved. One night, I shared that I was considering starting a caregiver support group. Sue caught my eye from across the room and mouthed, *I want to do this with you.* That's when our friendship really began.

Sue was a caregiver, too. She and her husband shared a home with her mother, so right away, we were kindred spirits. For the next couple of years, we facilitated a group, meeting once a month with other caregivers to offer support to one another and to work through the heartaches and troubles of our situations.

Sue and I discovered that we had more in common than just caregiving, and we got together at other times, too, along with our spouses. We shared family times with our parents, and we enjoyed the kids-out-of-school freedom caregivers experience when they can manage to get away for a little while. Most of all, though, Sue and I enjoyed breakfast. Every two or three weeks, we slipped away for a couple of hours and met at a local coffee shop where we shared our hearts and our hurts, our successes and our failures. We laughed and cried and prayed—and ate. Calories didn't count on those days, and we often indulged in artery-clogging skillets of potatoes and eggs and sausage accompanied by stacks of pancakes with *real* syrup—none of that sugar-free stuff.

Sue always had a beautiful smile, but sometimes, a certain sadness in her eyes hinted at the burden she carried. One morning, though, there was not a hint of sadness. There was a sparkle and an excitement in her eyes that perfectly matched the smile. I couldn't wait to hear what was up.

"I had the most wonderful experience this week while I was walking with Sophie," she said after we had settled into a booth and given our order to the waitress. Sophie was Sue's championship Schnauzer and (almost) constant companion.

"We were taking our normal route through the neighborhood, and we were approaching a section of the sidewalk that always irritates me. There are crepe myrtles on either side of the walk, and the owners don't keep them trimmed. The branches hang out so you have to push them aside to pass, and some of the lower ones cover the walk so you have to step over them. I've always approached that section of the walk grumbling and complaining about inconsiderate people and irresponsible homeowners, but this morning was different. This morning, I looked up as I approached the crepe myrtles and was startled at how beautiful the rose-colored blossoms were, at what an elegant archway they formed for Sophie and me to pass through. And in the background, a little behind the crepe myrtles, was a tree *covered* with morning glories. I *love* morning glories, but I had never noticed them because I was so preoccupied with the crepe myrtles."

Her enthusiasm was contagious, and we spent a good bit of the morning talking about what a difference a change in perspective can make in your attitude. That was several years before Mom and Dad moved into assisted living, but I thought of that conversation often as Mom continued to slip away.

Alzheimer's is an insidious disease, but in some cases, it can have a "bright" side. Mom had lived a lot of her life in fear—fear of rejection, fear of criticism, fear of saying or doing the wrong thing. There were times when she shut herself off from friends and all but a select few family members, turning down invitations, eventually isolating herself from almost all social interaction because of her fears. However, as her memory faded, she forgot to be afraid. Her love of people and human contact emerged, and if anyone said "go," she was ready. She was not able to go much as her body weakened, but her fears were still gone, and her sweet smile and generous hugs still made her a favorite of those around her.

I'm not a Pollyanna, and I don't see the silver lining in every cloud. I've lived long enough, and am realistic enough, to realize that there are bad situations in life that no amount of perspective can change. Still, there are *those* times—those times when you raise your eyes from the untrimmed, almost impassable walkway and say, "Oh, there are morning glories. I love morning glories."

CHAPTER 43
Calling In Hospice Is Not Giving Up

Hebrews 9:27 *And as it is appointed unto men once to die.*

I didn't know much about hospice before Mom died. Hospice was called the year before when Dad had his stroke, but he went so quickly I didn't learn much about hospice and what its purpose was. All I knew was that, the day Dad died, the hospice nurse called the proper people to handle the necessary paperwork. I showed my ignorance in a short conversation with her.

"I guess this makes your job a little less heart-wrenching, when the patient doesn't linger for a long time."

"Oh, no," she said. "I hate it when they die quickly before I have a chance to get to help them. I worked with a patient recently who, at first, was in so much pain that he couldn't get out of bed. More than anything he wanted to see his grandson play soccer. We were able to make that happen. Hospice doesn't help a patient die but rather helps him make the most of the time he has left."

That experience should have left me more prepared when Mom's time came, but it didn't. She was in the advanced stages of Alzheimer's, but she was physically healthy. Then, she developed that skin condition with the long Latin name, along with the secondary infections that resulted in protracted hospital stays.

In a very short time, Mom could no longer get out of bed without help and had to be propped up to sit in a chair for a few minutes. Still, when the physical therapist told me there was nothing more she could do for Mom because she wasn't able to respond, I didn't listen. I clung to the hope that, when the infections were brought under control, Mom would get her strength back and things would go back to "normal."

I didn't accept the fact that the treatments she was receiving were doing more harm than good. Mom pulled out so many IVs that her veins collapsed, and she cried from the pain when the nurses tried to find another one. A surgeon put in a PICC line, but after he put in the third one, he said he couldn't put in another one if she pulled it out again.

The charge nurse on Mom's floor was very understanding and very patient. She listened to my concerns and answered my questions, and one day, she asked if we would consider talking with hospice. I didn't hear that, either, at first, but after I recovered from the shock, I began to ask questions and to listen. My brother and I, along with our supportive spouses, made an appointment to meet with a hospice representative.

It was hard to hear his words, even though he said them with extreme gentleness, and, as I mentioned before, it was even harder to watch him write Mom's name on the forms. It felt like we were not fighting hard enough, but the more we talked and the more we learned about the process, the more I realized that we were focusing on giving Mom the best quality of life in the time that was left to her.

Hospice worked with Mom's care facility, so she was able to return to familiar surroundings with familiar people. They provided a hospital bed that was placed in her cozy little room where she was surrounded by her favorite things. They provided a *Geri* chair so she could spend time in the common areas with other patients. The focus switched from curative treatments which were often cold, sterile, frightening, and painful to care that was filled with love, support, and comfort.

I lived in another state, but during my limited visits, I observed the tender care she was given by the hospice nurse who came in to check on Mom each day. I also watched another caregiver carefully chop Mom's food and keep up a cheerful one-sided conversation as she fed her.

Calling in hospice felt like giving up, but it wasn't. It was the next step in the natural process of life, which, one way or another, eventually comes to an end.

CHAPTER 44
Mom's Shrinking Life

John 3:30 *He must increase, but I must decrease.*

Mom's condition continued to deteriorate, and I counted the days until I could see her again. As my April birthday approached, I announced that I wanted to spend my special day with my mom. I called Aunt Fay and invited her to join us, and we planned another visit.

I couldn't wait to see Mom again, but I dreaded it at the same time. There was less of her each time I saw her. I'm not talking about physical size, although she was losing weight since she couldn't feed herself and couldn't graze off the plates of her tablemates, but her life was getting smaller and smaller.

This shrinking phenomenon had started years before, when Alzheimer's first made its presence obvious in her life. She never "lived life large." She was too shy and fearful. She worked outside the home for twenty years, but the exposure was sometimes overwhelming, and she spent her evenings recovering in the security of her darkened bedroom. She and Dad traveled some, too, making one tour of the Holy Land and another to Germany to see the *Passion Play* at Oberammergau, but her social anxiety overshadowed a lot of the enjoyment.

After retirement, she and Dad moved to Carrollton, Texas, to be closer to me and my family. She found security in routines and ventured out to the familiar territory around their small, two-bedroom home. On shopping day, she browsed the bargain racks at Marshall's, Ross, and T.J. Maxx. She went to the library and ended her outing at the supermarket. She enjoyed the greetings of the clerks and sales people she met, because they were friendly but didn't demand anything in return.

As the Alzheimer's progressed, the routine became less secure. The city streets and store aisles were no longer familiar, choosing books was confusing, and the grocery list was indecipherable, so she gave up her independence. Instead of driving herself, she rode in the passenger seat on her occasional outings, and she stayed in the safety of home the majority of the time.

As she and Dad slid down the slippery slope of dementia together, they moved in with us, and her world became even smaller. She enjoyed their in-law apartment, but having her in my home gave me a ringside seat to the heartbreaking process. Unable to read any longer, she spent most of her time sitting on the sofa, dozing or watching TV. She lost the ability to carry out simple tasks like setting the table and rinsing the dishes, and she needed help with personal things like bathing and dressing. She had trouble remembering people and events, and she often talked about me rather than to me. She was sweet and loving and mostly compliant, but as her world became smaller, my load increased. When I reached my breaking point, and she and Dad moved into an assisted living facility, the real shrinkage began.

Their apartment was tiny, but they had their own furniture and knickknacks, and they had each other, so they were content. We tried an outing for ice cream once when I was there for a visit, but getting them in and out of the van proved to be a negative on the cost/benefit scale. From then on, their world consisted of walks to the dining room and back and an occasional trip to the common area for exercise or entertainment of some sort. Mom still recognized Dad and Jim, and she greeted me with what seemed to be some recognition, but she called all the blonde, female staff members Linda.

Her world changed drastically when Dad passed away. We worried that she would fall apart, but in this case, Alzheimer's continued to be a blessing, and she no longer remembered her companion of seventy years. For a few months, she thrived and became quite the party girl, greeting everyone she met with a beautiful smile that made her eyes sparkle and open arms that invited a warm hug. She needed help walking, but that was no problem since the staff loved her, and all the aids were glad for the opportunity to spend a few minutes with her. She was the belle of the ball at her ninetieth birthday party, even though she had no idea what was going on, and she kept everyone at our table laughing at the New Year's dinner.

Then, the skin outbreak came, along with the UTIs, the pneumonia, and over fifty days in the hospital. She became too weak to walk, but her bright smile remained, and another staff of caregivers fell in love with her sweet spirit. She didn't remember names, but she referred to Jim as "my boy," and she responded to me with recognition of some special connection. She laughed at Jim's teasing and clapped and hummed when he played the guitar—but she was so much smaller than before.

When her body failed to respond to treatment, she was moved back to Southridge under hospice care. She had a studio apartment in the Alzheimer's wing. It was large enough to include a couple of chairs for visitors, and she still had her own things except for the hospital bed. She had a Geri chair, a sort of lounge chair on wheels, and she sat in it most of the day. It made it easier for the hospice nurse to feed her, it helped keep her lungs clear, and it allowed her to spend time in the common area with other residents.

That's where she was when I arrived for my birthday visit—in the common area, sitting in her Geri chair in front of the TV. She was asleep with one eye half open and one hand raised in the air. It was hard to rouse her, and when she woke up, her eyes were blank. During a couple of our subsequent visits, she was a little more responsive. One day, she told me I looked pretty, and when Aunt Fay said, "I love you," she responded with, "I love you, too." She occasionally held out her arms to be hugged, but there was no strength in her embrace, and her smile was not as wide and bright as it had been. As I sat holding her cool hand and stroking her smooth cheek that belied her ninety years, I thought about what John the Baptist had said when his disciples asked about Jesus' new ministry. Even one of the pillars of the Christian faith had faced a shrinking life in the end.

As Mom neared the end of her life, I wondered if she had a greater awareness of God. She had always had a strong faith, and even in her moments of greatest fear, she leaned on Him.

Before we left, Aunt Fay asked Mom a question.

"Have you seen any angels?" she said.

Mom shook her head no.

"Would you like a band of angels around you?"

She nodded.

We held her hands and Fay prayed that God would give His angels charge over her—that as she became less to us, that He would become more to her. That was the last time I saw Mom alive.

SECTION VI
Mom's Goodbye

CHAPTER 45
The Horror of Alzheimer's

1 Corinthians 15:55 *O death, where is thy sting? O grave, where is thy victory?*

As a blogger, I am sometimes asked to write a guest post for other bloggers. Even though I write principally about caregiving, faith, and family, it's important to me that any guest post I write be compatible with the theme of the blog where it will appear. One request came from a friend who has a blog called *Kompletely Krista*. I sat in front of my mental drawing board and mulled over how Krista described what she wrote—dark fantasy, paranormal, horror. That sounded like a perfect description of Alzheimer's.

As I frequently do before beginning a new project, I went to the internet to be sure I understood all the terms I would be dealing with. One of the definitions I found of *paranormal* involved phenomena such as telekinesis or clairvoyance. As far as I was aware, there were no cases of Alzheimer's involving telekinesis or clairvoyance, but the disease was certainly beyond current scientific understanding at that time. Plaque-encrusted nerve tangles seemed to be involved in the development of Alzheimer's, but their exact role wasn't understood. Strides were being made in slowing the progress of the disease, but at that point, there was no known cure.

I didn't have to look up dark fantasy to see how it related to Alzheimer's. Mom started having delusions before she and Dad moved in with us. One evening, David was supposed to pick her up and bring her to the church where I planned to meet them for dinner. Shortly after I arrived, I got a phone call from my frustrated husband.

"Would you please call your mother and tell her to open the door. She won't let me in."

I called and asked Mom what was going on. She spun a wild tale that doesn't bear repeating and calmed down only after I went to her house and let myself in with my key.

Later, after we had combined households, I frequently came home from work to her tales of phone calls Dad had received from old girlfriends. More than once, I was awakened by a knock on my bedroom door and a tearful revelation that Dad had run off with some unknown hussy when, in fact, he had gone to the bathroom. Thankfully, the dark fantasies came to an end when the neurologist prescribed the proper medication.

Mom's disease came on slowly, taking tiny bits of her memory over a fifteen-year span. Her mother died from the mind-wasting disease after eight years of lying in a bed, unaware of her surroundings, and Mom was aware enough for many years to know she faced the same fate. There were times when the horror of her future was too much, and she broke down and sobbed that she would rather die than live like her mother.

As her memory faded along with her fears, she no longer remembered that she was ill. She became sweet and childlike, enjoying the moment and delighting in the attention she received from her caregivers. Sadly, those of us she left behind in the real world still knew. I suffered the agony of watching the mother I knew become dependent on me for everything from medications to baths and even clean underwear. After she moved into assisted living and I didn't see her for weeks on end, the changes between visits were heartbreaking. I watched in horror as she slowly lost the ability to walk, to feed herself, to communicate much beyond a smile, a hug, and a few jumbled words.

Still, Alzheimer's didn't win. My last visit with her was a month before she died. Most of the time I was with her, she was asleep or vacant, but one morning, her eyes cleared as she looked at me and said, "You look pretty today." She still lit up when my brother came to visit, and she clapped when he played his guitar for her. Her faith was strong, and up to the end, the nurses said she hummed along to the old gospel hymns she heard on TV.

The day Mom died was a good day. She smiled and giggled at the therapy dog one of the nurses brought to see her, and she ate everything the hospice nurse fed her. Shortly after dinner, an orderly put her to bed, and two hours later, when the charge nurse made her normal rounds, Mom was lying there with a peaceful smile on her face, and she was gone.

I like to think that, as she slept, she felt a gentle hand on her shoulder. She opened her eyes and saw Jesus on one side of her bed and Dad on the other. Then, she heard a soft voice.

"Helen, wake up. You've had enough of this horror. Let's go home."

CHAPTER 46
The Cycle of Life

Ecclesiastes 3:1 *To every thing there is a season, and a time to every purpose under the heaven.*

On May 24, 2012, we laid Mom to rest. We celebrated her life with a simple but heartfelt memorial service attended by a few relatives and close friends. It was the feminine version of the service we had held for Dad one year and one week before.

We knew what to expect the second time around, so many of the decisions were easier. Both Dad and Mom had pre-need funeral policies, so her body was transported from Conway to Dallas for burial. Her casket choice was detailed in the paperwork, and the marker was already in place on the lawn crypt she was to share with Dad. All it lacked was her date of death. She had made the service choices simple, too, by leaving handwritten instructions about the songs and scripture she wanted used. She had asked for one simple flower arrangement from the family, and she had listed charities to receive donations in lieu of flowers.

Although she didn't specify, there was little question about what she would wear. She had a cobalt blue party dress she'd bought for her golden wedding anniversary celebration, and she loved it. She wore it as often as possible after that. It became her uniform for weddings of grandchildren and other festive occasions. Somehow, she managed to avoid spilling wedding cake or punch on it, so it still looked new.

There was one decision to be made when Jo Lynn realized she had forgotten to bring jewelry. I went through mine and found some dangly rhinestone earrings and a simple rhinestone necklace that I hadn't worn in decades and probably never would again. First, the earrings were clip-ons, which I can't tolerate any more, and second, rhinestones don't go with jeans, even dress jeans. I showed my selections to Jo Lynn, and she agreed they were the perfect amount of bling.

On the day of the service, we gathered in the same beautiful chapel where we had said goodbye to Dad the previous year. The casket Mom had chosen didn't arrive in time, so the funeral home gave her an upgrade. The original model was white with a pale pink lining. The upgrade had some beautiful brass accents added to the outside, and it had a pink flower embroidered on the lining of the lid and another on the blanket—a little added bling. She looked beautiful, not really like Mom, but the care staff had followed instructions and applied her makeup with a light touch. Her dress draped perfectly, her jewelry sparkled at her neck and ears, and her hands rested in a perfectly natural pose.

After a time of visiting and looking at photo albums Jo Lynn had made over the years, we took our seats for the service. In another season of his life, Jim had sung in a gospel quartet, and Mom had loved their music. One of the songs she had requested was "He Touched Me." Jim had a recording the quartet had made of that song, and we played it for her. The other song she wanted was "Precious Lord, Take My Hand," and Jim's son, Sean, sang that. Pastor Rolen from our church officiated and read Psalm 116, also her choice. He focused on verse 15 which says:

Precious in the sight of the Lord is the death of His saints.

I never really understood that verse, but Pastor Rolen explained that it's a matter of perspective. While we see death as an ending, from God's perspective, it's a beginning, a homecoming.

After a brief time at the gravesite where we committed Mom's body to the dust from which it came, the funeral director had a few things to give us. There was the guest book, some thank you cards to be used in acknowledging all the kindnesses we had been shown, and a couple of floral gifts. One was a basket of flowers from Jo Lynn's sister, and the other was a potted peace lily from Aunt Fay's church. We decided I would take the lily and she would take the flowers.

"I don't have any place to put another plant," she said, "and I have lots of peace lilies from other funerals."

Maybe all those funerals were a result of being a minister's wife, or maybe it was an indication of where we were in the cycle of life. Pastor Rolen opened the service with the passage from the third chapter of Ecclesiastes that says there is a season for everything under heaven. There was a season in my life when a majority of my social events were graduation-related followed closely by a series of wedding-related events. During that season, a large section of my closet was filled with bridesmaid dresses. The next season was full of baby showers followed a few years later by a repeat of the graduation and wedding cycles. Finally, I had entered the funeral cycle. As my friends and family aged, I was becoming more familiar with the end of the cycle.

Still, it's a cycle, so there really is no end. The two songs Mom chose talked about God's touch. One says, "He touched me, and now I am no longer the same," and the other says, "Precious Lord, take my hand, lead me on." Pastor Rolen shared one more story about Mom. When she was in her early teens, she went to a brush arbor meeting. At that meeting, she asked God to touch her, and He did. Because of that touch, I wasn't seeing the end of Mom's cycle but rather the beginning of the next part of her cycle. Precious Lord, take her hand.

CHAPTER 47
Southridge Village's Tribute to Mom

Hebrews 6:10 For God *is not unrighteous to forget your work and labour of love, which ye have shewed toward his name, in that ye have ministered to the saints, and do minister.*

After Mom died, we received a lot of sweet, heartfelt expressions of sympathy. There were e-mails, notes on Facebook, cards, phone calls, and personal words of support. All of them meant so much and helped us deal with the grief, but none of them meant more to me than the one we received from Southridge Village.

Mom spent the last seventeen months of her life at Southridge. Her nails were not always clipped the way I would have done it, but she was always clean and well dressed. There were sometimes dust bunnies under her sofa, but she always had a smile on her face and seemed to feel secure and happy there. It broke my heart when I could no longer care for her in my home, but the staff at Southridge made it a little easier to let go, and they cared for her in ways I couldn't. Besides, I knew they cared about Mom not just as a resident but also as a person. They always greeted her with real smiles and generous hugs. They sometimes lingered with her even after her needs had been met, and when I visited, it was sometimes hard to tell who was family and who was staff.

A week after the funeral, we got a card from Southridge. The printed verse was very nice in a Hallmark kind of way. What meant the most, though, was the scattering of handwritten notes in the card. There were the usual expressions of sorrow for our loss and assurances of thoughts and prayers, but there was more. There were little messages that spoke of how Mom had touched them, how in spite of the Alzheimer's, they had connected with her. Here are some of my favorites:

I'm going to miss walking down the hall and seeing your mother's smiling face!

Your mother was so precious!

I'll never forget dancing with her on [wing] 300 and listening to her hum to the songs at church. Her place is next to Jesus, and we will remember her smile every day.

I will miss your mother's smiling face. She was an amazing lady with great spirits.

Your mom was a great woman.

Mrs. Robinson was an angel, always smiling and so cheerful. She will be greatly missed.

We will miss her sweet smiles every day.

I loved Helen's smile.

Mrs. Robinson was truly a blessing to know and love. I am glad to have been a part of her life.

She was a true joy and blessing to have.

Some researchers believe that people with Alzheimer's develop something they call emotional contagion which causes them to be greatly affected by the emotional state of their caregivers. Our family was blessed that our choice of a residential care facility included a staff that was not only well-qualified and efficient but also positive, loving, and caring.

CHAPTER 48
I Miss My Mom

Psalm 35:14 *I bowed down heavily, as one that mourneth for his mother.*

I miss Mom. I've missed her for a long time. For most of my life, I talked to her almost every day, but after Alzheimer's invaded her mind, those talks gradually lost their meaning.

Mom was smart, but she was never an intellectual. She didn't care much about politics, philosophy, or current events. She cared about her family and the things that affected our lives directly.

She went to work outside our home when I was in third grade, and Jim and I became latchkey kids. It was a gentler time when children played outside unsupervised and walked or rode their bikes to school without fear. Still, Mom was cautious. We were required to stay inside when she and Dad were at work, and I was required to call her when I arrived home from school.

It was supposed to be a brief check-in to let her know I was safe, but it became a special time between mother and daughter. She shared funny stories about her day on the switchboard and her latest frustrations with the office harridan, and I shared the latest playground escapades and test grades. In junior high and high school, my daily reports expanded to include the joys and sorrows of puppy love.

After I graduated and went away to college, our daily talks stopped for a while. There were no cell phones then, and our limited family budget didn't stretch far enough to cover many long-distance calls. After a year, I dropped out and moved back home to work for a while, and the calls resumed. I called her on my lunch hour to bring her up to date on the latest office gossip and, later on, the latest antics of the cute guy whose desk I passed several times a day on my way to deliver files or pick up mail.

When I married him, the calls continued as I asked advice on setting up housekeeping, cooking, and other newlywed issues. When I quit work to start a family, our conversations turned to baby subjects and the intrigues of our favorite soap operas. The calls continued through my divorce and my learning-to-be-single years. Then, when I dived back into the dating pool, we cycled back to the joys and sorrows of a more mature kind of love.

Through all of it, she was always a good listener, a sympathetic ear who usually took my side, and she was always there when I needed her. Then, she started to slip away. She found it difficult to follow the subject of our conversation, and she began to have trouble keeping the characters straight, both in the soaps and in our lives. Alzheimer's came between us and stole away the history we had built together, and I missed her.

When she and Dad moved in with us, I saw her every day, and we spoke often, but we didn't really talk. There were flashes of her old personality, but her disease had changed her from my mother and lifelong confidante into a needy child who depended on me for her security.

Shortly after she left my home and moved into assisted living, we tried a speaker phone conference call. Unfortunately, she couldn't understand where that disembodied voice came from, and she didn't know how to respond. We didn't try any more calls after that.

I visited her every two or three months, and I sat and held her hand while we watched TV. I told her I loved her, and she said she loved me, but I'm not sure she knew who I was.

Now she's gone, and she's whole in mind and spirit. I wish I could talk to her, but I know she's busy catching up on all the heavenly gossip. I miss her every day, but not as much as I did when she was still here.

CHAPTER 49
Feeling the Emptiness

Proverbs 24:3–4 *³Through wisdom is an house builded; and by understanding it is established: ⁴And by knowledge shall the chambers be filled with all precious and pleasant riches.*

Christian was seventeen years old when his dad and I separated, and he took it pretty hard. For the first few days, he stayed with his dad, but that didn't work out very well. I was temporarily staying with Mom and Dad, so he came over to bunk with us. The first night, we sat up late talking through our grief and fear. At one point, he asked where *his* home would be. I don't think I really understood what he was feeling until a few weeks after Mom passed away.

Jim and Jo Lynn had a garage sale to dispose of as many of Mom and Dad's worldly possessions as possible. Whatever was not sold was to be donated to charity, and all we had left was the few things we had each chosen as keepsakes. I didn't think it would matter a lot to me. I had disposed of some of their things along with a lot of mine and David's when we moved to Florida, and I gave away a truckload of our combined material excess when we left Florida. During all the transitions, I felt the usual discomforts that come with life changes, but I didn't feel the deep, empty melancholy I felt after that garage sale. I left Mom and Dad's home when I was nineteen years old, but that garage sale disposing of the last of their earthly goods made that break final. The little house they lived in before they moved in with David and me wasn't "home" because I had never lived there. Their half of the house in Florida was attached to, but not really a part of, my home, and their apartment in the assisted living facility wasn't home, either. Still, all three were places where my Mom and Dad lived, and they represented home to me.

Once they were both gone, all that was left were the pieces of wood and fabric they'd sat and slept on, the knickknacks they'd collected and dusted, and the pictures they'd admired. Those things held no life of their own, but they held a lot of memories. I still had the memories, but the rest of it was gone.

Except for the two weeks after my marriage broke up, I had lived in a home of my own since I was nineteen. All the same, there was always someplace where I could go, someplace where Mom and Dad were, someplace where I could remember what it was like to be a child, to be taken care of, to turn the responsibility over to someone else. I guess that's what Christian was wondering, where he would go to get that feeling when he needed it. I don't know if he found it in the homes I have made since then. Probably not since his whole family wasn't there. After all those years, I finally understood the emptiness he must have felt, because I felt it, too.

CHAPTER 50
Freedom's Just another Word for Nothing Left to Write

Ecclesiastes 3:22 *Wherefore I perceive that there is nothing better, than that a man should rejoice in his own works.*

On the drive home from Mom's funeral, I looked out the window at the passing scenery and wanted to go home, pack up the RV, and head out. Along with the sadness and loss, I felt the lifting of a burden, of a years-long task finally completed, and I wanted to live out that freedom on the open road. It wasn't a good time, though. Finances were tight, and we had responsibilities we couldn't drop at a moment's notice. Still, short jaunts were doable, so, a few weeks later, we drove to Louisiana to celebrate the Fourth of July with David's family.

It was a week of focusing on freedom, on its meaning and its price. It was a week of experiencing personal freedom for me, freedom from worrying about how Mom was doing, from the nagging guilt that is the caregiver's constant companion, from the fear of the dreaded phone call. It was a week of thinking about the freedoms Mom and Dad had attained, freedom from the bonds of dementia and the pains and limitations of old age. Unfortunately, freedom can have its down side.

Trips had become a source of a lot of writing material for me. I had written about the adventures and misadventures of traveling with Mom and Dad as well as the uneasiness of traveling without them. I had written about the heart-wrenching visits to Arkansas, watching first Dad and then Mom slip away—but this trip was different. There was no one to prepare for but myself, no concern about leaving duties unattended to, no anxiety about what I'd find when I got where we were going. It was almost a perfect trip, but there was something missing. I didn't have anything to write about.

There were still stories to tell, funny and touching stories about family get-togethers, shopping trips, and honey-dos for David to do for his mom—but the muse wasn't there. The angst that usually drove me to the keyboard was missing, and I experienced what all writers fear more than a rejection letter—writer's block. Was it a temporary setback, or was it permanent? Would the words come back, or had I written them all?

I didn't really believe it was a serious block, but I tend to be a bit of a drama queen in the recesses of my mind, so I fretted over the possibility a bit. I did a little editing work, but I didn't finish much. When we returned home, I puttered on the keyboard a bit, but mostly, I fretted over my lack of productivity.

When I first started writing, I had some of the same productivity issues. I started a lot of projects that took a long time to finish. My first book took four years and fourteen edits to complete. I had help and encouragement from people with a lot more experience than I had. One thing they encouraged me to do was to find my voice. Voice has to do with choice of style and words, but it also has to do with perspective. Up to that point, I had written from the perspective of anxiety, turmoil, and unfinished business, but after my caregiving came to an end, I began to write from a place of peace, calm, and closure. I continued to focus on caregiving, faith, and family, but I also sought to enlarge my territory.

I knew there was plenty left to write about and lots of new territory to explore. Now, I had the freedom to find my new voice and to pursue those words that were hiding somewhere behind the grief.

CHAPTER 51
Just Let Me Feel Bad

Matthew 26:38 *Then saith he unto them, My soul is exceeding sorrowful, even unto death: tarry ye here, and watch with me.*

One morning, not long after the garage sale, I couldn't settle on a task in the house, so I went outside to help David deal with the two dead trees he had felled earlier in the week. He had become a real Paul Bunyan, except with a chain saw instead of an axe.

Stacking logs and piling up limbs took a lot of physical effort, but it left my mind free to wander. I had gone through my prayer list a little earlier, and I began thinking of all the sad things that had happened in the three weeks since Mom died. Three friends had lost their moms, my aunt had lost her best friend, and another friend had lost her son. At least three friends had parents who were in their final stages, and three more were battling a recurrence of cancer. As I pondered all the tragedies, I wondered how I could best help and support my friends who were going through trying times.

When I was growing up, my family didn't deal well with emotions; in fact, we didn't deal with them at all. We denied, avoided, and otherwise swept them under the proverbial rug. As a result, I feared emotions and made it my mission in life to be sure everyone I knew was in a constant state of euphoria. I was the queen of *Don't feel bad—just smile and it will be all better.* After lots of counseling experience, both as a counselor and a counselee, I learned that my method didn't work. The bad feelings were there because it was a bad situation, and feeling bad was part of the healing process. That morning as I worked, I continued to think about the subject, but I didn't come to any conclusions.

After a couple of hours of dealing with dead wood, David and I cleaned up and went to the Senior Center for lunch. One of the regular ladies has a beautiful voice and loves to sing, and sometimes, she brings her boom box and serenades us. That was one of those days, and she sang a number of old-time gospel songs, all of which seemed to be about Mama and Heaven. It wasn't long before my tears were flowing. Some were tears of sadness and loneliness, and some were tears of joy that Mom was "all better," but all were tears of healing. Nobody took much notice. My friend across the table shed some tears of her own, partly sharing in my grief but partly remembering her own mother and the child she'd lost way too soon. David brought me a dry napkin when mine became a soggy mess, and he draped his arm gently around my shoulder—but nobody told me not to cry.

When it was time to leave, I went over and hugged the singer. She had seen my tears and held me in a comforting embrace.

"You know, we buried my Mom three weeks ago," I said.

"I'm sorry. I didn't know."

Then, she listened as I told her a few stories about Mom, and she shared a couple of stories of her own. As we bonded in the sisterhood of grief, I felt validated and affirmed.

After I returned home, my eyes felt scratchy and puffy, and I felt drained. At the same time, I felt strengthened. I knew I would cry more tears and feel more grief, but in time, I knew the wound of Mom's loss would become a scar, evidence of the healing that had taken place. Even now, I continue to tell my stories, and sometimes, I cry—and when sorrows come to those I know, I bring them dry napkins, listen to their stories, and offer a shoulder for them to cry on.

CHAPTER 52
I Miss Mom When I Pray

2 Samuel 12:23 *But now he is dead, wherefore should I fast? Can I bring him back again? I shall go to him, but he shall not return to me.*

I wrote earlier about how much I missed my frequent talks with Mom, but there were so many other ways that I missed her. When she first moved from my home into assisted living, I missed her presence in the back seat of the car. It wasn't the emotional kind of missing that makes your heart hurt but, rather, a something's-not-there kind of missing, more like what I imagine an amputee might feel when he or she experiences phantom pain. It was nice not to have to worry about anyone's seat belt but my own, and it was even nicer not to have to answer repeated questions about where we were going, why we were going, and when we would get there, but there was still the occasional feeling that I needed to turn around and check to be sure she was okay.

Special occasions were hard, too, especially the first ones. Her birthday without her was difficult, Christmas preparations were tinged with sadness as I realized there was one less name on the gift list, and Mother's Day was lonely. I had experienced a lot of loss in my life, though, and I had counseled and comforted others in their times of loss, so I knew what to expect. Still, there was one unexpected time when I missed Mom—when I prayed.

One night, I was lying in bed, praying silently. There were no soaring, inspiring words; it was more of a *now-I-lay-me-down-to-sleep* kind of prayer, whispered in the recesses of my mind as I hovered in the limbo between wakefulness and sleep. When I got to the *God bless* part, I remembered friends and family who were going through physical and emotional struggles, and as I edged closer to that drop-off into the abyss, I thought *God, please be with Mom.* Suddenly, my mind jerked me back from the brink. *Wait a minute. Mom is already there, in the place where there is no pain, no tears, no sorrow.* Even in my foggy state of mind, I felt not only a sense of gratitude but also a sense of emptiness and loss—gratitude that Mom had passed beyond her confusion and suffering, but emptiness because of the loss of a special kind of connection.

I will carry Mom's memory with me always, and I believe I will be reunited with her when my time comes, but for now, she no longer needs my prayers. That night, I felt God smiling indulgently at His sleepy child, and I smiled sheepishly in return. *Well,* I sighed just before I slipped into unconsciousness, *can You please tell her hello and that I love her.*

CHAPTER 53
Loss and Gain

Philippians 1:21 *For to me to live is Christ, and to die is gain.*

After a friend and fellow caregiver returned from caring for a loved one in distress, she and I exchanged several e-mails. In addition to travel fatigue, she was feeling especially sad because of the approaching anniversary of the death of someone who had played a major role in her life. One of her e-mails was short and to the point.

"It's been a pretty tough week. Jet lag and grief apparently enhance one another."

I had seen a lot of grief around me during that time. Perhaps it was because of that cycle of life thing, when losses begin to occur more frequently—or perhaps, as popular eschatology speculates, it's the times in which we live. Regardless of the cause, I was seeing many people who were suffering loss: loss of loved ones through death; loss of relationships through other causes; loss of career, security, home; loss of health and independence; loss of innocence and trust; loss of hopes and dreams.

My e-mail friend is also one of my manuscript readers. When she read the chapter about writer's block, she made the following comment:

"Loss and gain never travel separately, do they?"

That was certainly the case in the loss of Mom and Dad. Shortly after our Louisiana trip, David and I went to Branson with friends for a few days. As I prepared for the trip, I once again exulted in the freedom of not having to be sure all caregiving bases were covered in case of an emergency, but when we passed through Conway, Arkansas, it hurt, knowing that Mom and Dad weren't there. When we arrived at the condo in Branson, I thought about how hard it would have been for them to get up the stairs to the unit where we were staying. Once inside, I laughed to myself, thinking about how miserable they would have been in the seventy-degree air-conditioning, and how miserable they would make everyone else as a result.

There was a sense of freedom in knowing I didn't have to deal with those things, but there was a sense of loss as well. I felt similar moments of gain and loss throughout the trip. We went to places I had been with Mom and Dad that reminded me of another time when I was a child and they were young and healthy; and we went to difficult-to-negotiate places that reminded me of how limited their mobility was toward the end.

Experiencing loss brings up the difficult questions: why do bad things happen to good people, why didn't God stop it, why me, where's the gain? I don't have any answers, but the Apostle Paul addressed the subject.

Romans 8:28 *And we know that all things work together for good to them that love God, to them who are the called according to his purpose.*

To me, this doesn't mean that God causes bad things to happen, but when they do, He can use them for a good purpose if we let Him. Paul gives us a clue as to what one of those purposes might be.

2 Corinthians 1:3–4 ³ *Blessed be God, even the Father of our Lord Jesus Christ, the Father of mercies, and the God of all comfort;* ⁴ *Who comforteth us in all our tribulation, that we may be able to comfort them which are in any trouble, by the comfort wherewith we ourselves are comforted of God.*

This resonates with me because of my experiences in telling my stories. When people are helped or comforted by something I've written, it gives some meaning to the last few years of Mom and Dad's lives. However, as much as I like what Paul had to say, the words of Jesus mean the most. Isaiah's prophecies described Jesus as "a man of sorrows, acquainted with deepest grief," so He knows what we're going through. From this place of understanding, He made us a promise.

Matthew 5:4 *Blessed are they that mourn: for they shall be comforted.*

ABOUT THE AUTHOR

After years as a family caregiver, Linda began to write as a way of helping herself and others deal with the pain and frustration of caregiving. Now that her parents are eternally healed, she writes about life in the country, her feral Kitty, and her husband David.

Printed in Poland
by Amazon Fulfillment
Poland Sp. z o.o., Wrocław

53384167R00108